THE CHEQUERED LADY

And Other Tales from Australian Courts

Phil Kafcaloudes

Illustrated by
Gregg Arthur

Universal
Law Publishing Co. Pvt. Ltd.
NEW DELHI - INDIA

PREFACE

Australians have the most inventive ways of getting into trouble. As a legal reporter for ABC Radio, I have come across some cases that are hard to believe.

Incredible though they may seem, the tales in this collection were inspired by real events. But it should also be said that I did not intend the stories to be accurate renditions of actual cases. The circumstances of the cases have been substantially changed and all the names and places are fictional. Many of the characters are based on real people or composites of real people – but often these characterisations are largely works of imagination, as are many of the conversations used in the stories. It would be impossible, for example, to know what two police officers said to each other in the privacy of a patrol vehicle, or to know what a person is thinking at the time of a crime.

Why did I write this book? It's been said that although Australia is cosmopolitan, cultural crossovers within this country are limited. Four years of watching and reporting the activities of people in Australian Criminal, Summary and Civil Courts has proved to me that this adage is simply not true. We are a colourful bunch of individual personalities, and I'd like to pass on some of the entertainment.

Phil Kafcaloudes
August 1993

CONTENTS

The judge wasn't convinced. He asked the barrister to run through what the worker claimed happened on the day he was injured.

Russell Mackinolty was a coal miner at the Newcastle colliery. Like many workers, he lived in a housing estate established by the employer. It was only a few kilometres from the job site.

When he was employed, Russell was told to report to the above-ground job site at 6.30 every morning, and catch a forty-five-degree lift down to the cut surface.

For a few months Russell followed this procedure. But it was time consuming. By the time he walked to the elevator shaft and waited for the invariably late lift, it was usually seven o'clock – a waste of half-an-hour's valuable sleep.

In the long walk to the ground site every day, Russell walked past what looked like a conveyor belt which ran directly down a hatch into the ground.

He asked his supervisor what the belt was for, and was told it was used for the transport of coal, but was rarely operational. The supervisor said it was a shame, since it went from near their own underground worksite, up through the ground for two kilometres, coming out on the surface (where Russell passed it each day).

Yes, it was safe – the belting was still strong. In fact it was still turned on every month or so – just to check it was operational.

Russell continued to catch the lift every morning, but the lure of the easy walk down the conveyor dogged him. The conveyor was on a thirty-degree angle – shallow enough to walk on and maintain control.

Russell succumbed.

The first day was easier than he expected. The guiderails on each side of the wide conveyor belt were the perfect height to be used as handrails. The webbing material of the belt provided good grip for his workboots.

The walk down the two-kilometre belt was a quick tread – in fact he reached the face before he would have reached the above-ground elevator point if he had stayed on the surface.

For the next six months Russell travelled to work via the old conveyor belt. He checked every week when the belt was being tested – just to be sure it didn't start up while he was on it.

Russell had been extremely careful. He foresaw every possible problem – except for one.

The conveyor was dimly lit, but it was still clear enough for him to see ten or fifteen metres in front. However it was not bright enough for Russell to see a wet patch that had appeared on the belt. Directly above the belt was porous rock which allowed some seepage to drip – very little, but enough.

Russell was about three-quarters down the belt when he lost his footing on the wet webbing. At an angle of thirty degrees, any loss of control invariably means a rapid acceleration of forward progress. The miner fell on his backside after hitting the slippery part, and by the time he realised he was losing control, he was careering down the belt – getting exponentially faster.

Five hundred terrifying metres later the belt ended.

Suddenly.

Conveyor belts do that.

Russell's flight however did not end. The miner continued on, flying through the air over a congregation of startled miners and out of the door into the next workstation.

Any thoughts the workers may have had that this was a cosmic visitation from the great mining angel in heaven, ended with the loud crash from the next sector.

PETER: Why don't you stick a sign out the front asking for truckies to leave their fill down the back?

Two days later, down the road.

Jack Speilburg had been driving trucks for so long that he didn't notice the landscape any more. But today something on the side of the road up ahead caught his attention. A sign. A bright yellow sign, with the word "TRUCKIES" across the top.

"FILL WANTED".

Did it say fill wanted? He had tonnes of the stuff in his load. It was costing him an arm and a leg to get rid of it.

A minute later Jack was standing in front of the huge sign. They wanted fill. No charge. Just dump it around the back. Must be mad. Jack walked around the back. There was plenty of room for the truck. Must be a catch.

He went back to the sign. At the bottom were the words printed clearly: "NO CATCHES". You beauty.

For the next week Jack took every load of fill to the back of the house. One time he saw the old woman and waved guiltily. She smiled and waved back. So it was all right after all.

What a good lurk! He had saved hundreds by dumping at the site. Jack did feel a little guilty about not telling his mates. After all, they were in the same boat – paying out plenty because the council didn't have enough dumps. He decided to tell them about his free dump site. . . Sometime.

The Roadhouse Inn – a week later.

"Jackie boy!"

Jack waved to his mates. The same faces. It was like they lived at the roadhouse. They sat in the same places in the same clothes, day after day.

JACK: G'day Weasel. Snot. Tessa. Billy-boy.

ALL: Your shout Jackie!

JACK: Just my bloody timing!

Jack went to the bar. Long John was waiting for service. He never took part in a shout. He liked scotch. The boys were happy for him to buy his own.

JACK: How's it going Long?

LONG JOHN: Bloody awful Jackie. Mate, I'm losing money like crazy bro. I'm thinking about chucking it in. Selling the rig. Bloody crazy mate. Bills and more bills. . .

JACK: Whatch yer havin'? Jack rattled off his order, and then ordered another for Long.

LONG JOHN: No, mate really. I'll get me own.

JACK: Garbage, buddy. You need another. No debt.

Long rolled his half-empty drink in his palms, and then looked at the bottles lined up above the till.

LONG JOHN: I really think this is it, Jackie. It's nine-ter-five fer me.

Long's blues upset Jack. A truckie must really be down to think about dropping out of the game. Even when the missus walks out, most of the fraternity take it on the chin. A drunk night. . . A pickup. . . New girl. . . Maybe a bit of aggro for a while. . . But things all work out.

Jack knew what he had to do.

JACK: Mate, if you could get rid of your fill without having to pay, would it help?

LONG JOHN: Bloody oath!

Long looked ıt Jack hopefully.

JACK: All right then. I'll tell you. But mate, you can't tell anyone. Not even the fellas. If we overuse

The waving and calls resumed.

TED: Mervyn, you're a wimp!

Within a minute Ted was walking assuredly up to the old woman. Mervyn went inside to make a cup of tea. Ted soon came running back, ducking swings from a hoe.

That night the decision was made to make an official complaint.

The Supreme Court – six months later.

Justice Klein knew he must not laugh, and he quietly tapped his pen on the desk. Out of the side of his eye he was aware his associate was stifling the giggles. Damn. She knows what effect this has on him.

Must look serious.

He slicked his hair with his right hand, cleared his throat and pressed on.

> *JUSTICE KLEIN:* The prosecuting council has just estimated that the ten thousand cubic metres of fill will cost thirty-eight thousand dollars to remove. This is not insubstantial. But the fact remains that the woman allowed the fill to be placed on the property for almost two months. I asked the defendant why she did not do anything about it. All she could say was that she did not realise how much was being left by the trucks. I must say that I find this statement most perplexing. At the time of the complaint the mound of fill was five metres high and was wide enough to be spilling on properties on both sides. I can only conclude that she did know this was more than your average trailer load. In fact, I must go further. I don't believe Mrs Brewer really considered the effects the mounting fill was having on the neighbours. . .

VOICE: (From the back of the room.) You're bloody right!

By the time the courtroom looked around to see who interrupted, Ted was looking blankly ahead. The judge was thrown from his usual flowing style. The associate and the tipstaff were both shaking with repressed mirth.

In thirteen years on the bench, Jim Klein had had to deliver verdicts in some strange cases, but this one was the weirdest. Must soldier on.

JUDGE KLEIN: And so. . . the. . .

TED: (From the back of the room.) You were up to the neighbours!

The associate, tipstaff and the court recorder sprayed out chuckles. The sheriff's officer, always impassive, commanded silence. Order was restored.

JUDGE KLEIN: So taking all things into account, I agree with the orders proposed by the council – that you are to remove eighty-five percent of the fill at your own cost. The defendant is also to pay the very substantial costs of the proceedings. I'll adjourn the court.

He rose, shot a glare at his staff and retired.

Outside the courtroom Peter Brewer was under siege from his mother.

MRS BREWER: How are we going to get rid of ten thousand bloody things of dirt? You tell me, Einstein!

TED: You could put up another sign Mum – you know, "ANYONE WANTING SOME FREE FILL. . . "

HE'S GOOD WITH MONEY

This case just shows how a moment of temptation can corrupt the incorruptible. There are cases like this every day.

It was seven o'clock on a Tuesday night.

As usual, Peter Strait was working late. The bursar at a major university, Peter found the long hours were essential if he was to do his job properly.

He was constantly dealing with students who were tardy in their payments and missed deadlines – there wasn't enough time during normal working hours to deal with these problems.

Only two chores remained: to count the day's money (it had to be correct to the last cent) and then lock everything up. As usual, Peter carried this out meticulously. The money added up. The safe was locked and relocked, the files were put away, and the office closed.

He had done a thorough job. But it was now ten-to-eight. Peter only had ten minutes to get to the Greyhound Club to open the betting agency.

Because of his esteemed position within the university town, Peter had been asked to manage the local club's betting centre. The bursar considered this an honour.

He laid out the stubs, checked the float, set the television, and phoned on with the TAB. All was ready for a night's betting.

The first customer was Bluey, a regular. Peter started processing the bet. Blue, as was his custom, chatted through the whole thing.

"Geez, what a job takin' all the money. Must be some real rorts you blokes get up to."

Peter heard the same comments every week. At first he had been offended, but now he didn't care. “Besides”, Peter thought, “what kind of rort could I possibly get away with?”

Some people say Blue is telepathic. It certainly seemed so on this night, for Peter's thought was answered. “Easy, mate. You're not on computer link, so you can just bet for yerself *after* the race has finished. Use a false name, and no-one would know.”

Peter didn't respond, and just punched in the bets and returned the ticket to Blue. But as each race was run, Blue's suggestion came to mind. Temptation – that insidious stirring which has broken marriages and ruined careers – saddled Peter, egging this incorruptible man to change the ethic of a lifetime.

Race seven was the watershed. He waited until the race was run, and placed a bet on the ten-to-one winner. Terror and thrill.

Thrill for doing the unthinkable.

Terror for the fear of discovery.

And discovered it was. Peter did not know the TAB checked tickets. He was not aware the tickets were stamped with the issue time.

Peter was taken to court, convicted and fined. He also lost his highly paid job at the university. All because of an incomprehensible temptation. . . all for a six-dollar bet that he thought would win him sixty dollars.

JUST BAD LUCK

I have come to believe the adage: "truth is stranger than fiction". Courts are a reflection of events in society. And some of the coincidences revealed in courts would not be credible if they were coined from someone's imagination. This is one such case.

It was a Friday. Meryl had worked hard at her job all week, as well as shopping, looking after the kids, cleaning. . . She decided to have a day for herself.

Meryl rang her friend Bett and asked whether she would like to go to the city for the day. Bett had her own car, so they could do whatever they liked. Bett thought it was a marvellous idea.

Bett picked up Meryl, and the two women headed off for a day out.

Unfortunately, circumstance, and a car heading in the opposite direction, intervened.

Although Bett escaped unharmed, Meryl was taken to hospital and treated for a spinal injury. She was off work for a short time, and underwent some rehabilitation. It was a few months before she was able to resume her normal life.

Meryl went to court demanding the insurance company pay compensation for the injuries. A judge heard the evidence, found the crash to have been accidental, and awarded compensatory damages.

Twelve months after the accident, almost to the day, Meryl again thought how lovely it would be to go driving with her friend Bett.

Bett picked up Meryl and the pair headed off for a day together.

As the women were pulling out of the driveway, Meryl jokingly started to say that she hoped Bett would avoid all other cars this. . .

Unfortunately Meryl didn't get to finish the sentence. The doctors said the second, identical accident aggravated the earlier trauma. Meryl had injured the same part of the spinal column.

Meryl went back to court.

As was to be expected, the Supreme Court judge and the barristers on both sides were incredulous – and a little cynical. But the insurance company's doctors verified the fact that the second injury was genuine. Investigators concluded that neither accident had been fraudulently staged.

The judge said Meryl had suffered from extraordinarily bad luck, and awarded her forty thousand dollars for the injuries.

PS During the court case, Meryl was asked, under oath, to describe her problems. She answered (in all seriousness): "My sore neck. . . oh yes. . . and my husband. . ."

Sorry. The courts couldn't help her with that one. . .

THE TEQUILA MADE ME DO IT

Sydney, like all cosmopolitan cities, attracts people who have varying ideas of what constitutes "a good time". The following case demonstrates how tourists are capable of finding the most original ways of getting into trouble.

I walked into the media room after spending the morning chasing dead tips and hunches all over town. It was unusual. Not a win. Nothing for the mid-morning bulletins. I was desperate and frustrated. I threw my briefcase down on the desk and looked up at my colleague. His face told me he had struck gold.

"Okay. Tell me about it, Mike." I pulled my chair down to his end of the room and sat. Mike was so pleased with himself, this had to be a great yarn. Even his knee was shaking in glee.

"You won't believe me."

"Did you file the story?"

"Yep. Just finished."

"Well then it can't be true. But tell me anyway."

Apparently the paucity of stories had driven Mike and his colleague Jennie down to Central Court, the nemesis of the handbag snatcher, petty thief and flasher.

This was the building where many years ago someone in the public gallery slipped a gun to a notorious criminal, who in pique at a magistrate's unkind attitude, fired the weapon into the ceiling. The hole remains as a warning to testy beaks.

Indeed, many a sordid tale has been elucidated within these old walls.

Mike and Jennie took their places at the oak media table adjacent to the public gallery. Three young Japanese men were standing in the dock.

Magistrate "Red" Arthur was not in a good mood.

MAGISTRATE: Sergeant, who are the men in the dock?

SERGEANT: Charge cases four, five and six.

MAGISTRATE: Well that tells me a whole lot, doesn't it? Tell me what they're here for. . .

SERGEANT: (Knowing it's going to be one of those hard days.) This morning at approximately 5.10, Rose Bay police received a complaint that three men were acting in a most suspicious way near the main road.

A police car was dispatched to the alleged scene of the alleged crime. Information was received from a number of alleged bystanders.

At this point the two officers observed three naked male persons of oriental extraction running through the streets of Elizabeth Bay. The men were completely naked with the exception of their footwear.

The men were in the full view of people of all ages – both male and female – who were waiting at a nearby bus stop. The accused men were carrying a bottle of alcoholic beverage at the time.

Police investigations ascertained that the beverage referred to was, in fact, tequila.

MAGISTRATE: (To the men in the dock.) Do you want to plead?

Red Arthur was a magistrate from the old school which believed that if an accused was from another country, one only had to yell the question for the recipient to understand. The question was repeated – much louder. The men looked at each other, and mumbled among themselves for a moment. Two of the men pointed to the third, who moved to the front of the dock and bowed his head, then spoke in stilted but understandable English:

> *THIRD MAN:* Yes, Sir. We want to plead for mercy.
>
> *MAGISTRATE: (With some dramatic exasperation.)* No no no! Guilty or not guilty? Which one?
>
> *FIRST MAN: (Pushing the third man from behind.)* Guilty or not guilty, idiot!
>
> *THIRD MAN: (Bowing slightly.)* Guilty!

The third man bowed once more and sat down again.

> *MAGISTRATE: (To the second man.)* What about you?
>
> *SECOND MAN:* Guilty! *(More bowing.)*

The third had begun his guilty plea while the second was still bowing. The men all appeared very upset and extremely contrite.

Just then a legal aid solicitor charged into the court and announced, on the run, that he represented the three men in the dock.

Mr Arthur asked if the men had any explanation for their atrocious behaviour.

Yes. It seemed the trio were Japanese tourists and were due to leave Australia in the next few weeks. The solicitor said the men were very embarrassed by the episode and guaranteed there would not be a repeat of the Rose Bay show. They were respectable men and had never been in any trouble before. This incident had troubled the trio greatly. The magistrate was told of the shame that these men would carry with them back to their country.

Mr Arthur, taking into account the expressed contrition, decided to fine the men one hundred dollars each and allowed them to leave the court.

There was much gratitude on the part of the three men.

Outside, surrounded by Central's stony edifice, the trio's drawn faces and repentant slouches were replaced by rekindled gaiety.

Jennie asked the men what had led them to carry on in such a boisterous manner. Their dilemma was blamed on "the tequila".

Aware of the need of visual proof for her cynical readers, Jennie asked them if they would mind posing for a photograph.

The men looked at each other briefly and whipped off their shirts for the shots.

The men's offer to remove the rest of their clothing was not deemed necessary by the surprised journo. After all, they were in one of the city's busiest thoroughfares.

The trio were last seen gaily hopping off down Liverpool Street.

Hmm. Repentance don't last long. . .

EXPERT WITNESS

Sometimes the best prepared case can go horribly wrong. People just have this way of saying things on the witness stand that are completely unexpected.

A Sydney businessman sued a journalist claiming the journo had defamed him in a series of television features. One of the points which irked the businessman was the journalist's public ridicule of his knighthood.

In Australia knighthoods are bestowed on the recommendation of heads of government, but our businessman claimed he was given his gong by a group of gentlemen from Malta – the Knights of St John.

The television reporter alleged the businessman's knighthood was, in fact, paid for in cash and lacked credibility.

Preparation was the key to the success of this case. Simple preparation. The businessman had to find an expert on decorations, awards and the like, and ask this expert to give evidence on the stand.

This would convince the jury that the knighthood was genuine.

The businessman was confident. He had made contact with the leading expert in the field of knighthoods and decorations. The words "distinguished" and "unrivalled" were splashed around to describe this master on knighthoods.

The witness was put on the stand.

All started well. The expert told the jury the knighthood was genuine and respected. No amount of money could buy this knighthood. It must be earned.

It was one of the most sought-after decorations in the world.

The businessman sighed a breath of relief. His counsel sat down. Counsel and client looked at each other and winked. It was all over. Nothing could top that. His case was won.

Wrong.

Unfortunately for the businessman, the counsel for the journalist had also done his homework:

COUNSEL: How many medals do you yourself possess?

EXPERT: Oh, about sixty, Sir.

COUNSEL: Sixty?

EXPERT: About that, Sir.

COUNSEL: Name one of the awards.

EXPERT: The Iron Cross, Sir.

COUNSEL: The Iron Cross. Isn't the Iron Cross one of the most respected German awards?

EXPERT: I am proud to say that it is, Sir.

COUNSEL: When did you earn this Iron Cross.

EXPERT: In the War, Sir.

COUNSEL: Which war?

EXPERT: The big one, Sir. The Second World War.

COUNSEL: What were you doing in the Second World War.

EXPERT: I was a commander of a German PT boat, Sir.

COUNSEL: What year was this?

EXPERT: 1942, Sir.

COUNSEL: I see. How old are you now?

EXPERT: *(With a proud puffed chest.)* I am Sixty, Sir.

COUNSEL: Now let's see. In 1942, that would have made you thirteen years old. Are you saying that you were the commander of a German PT boat at the age of thirteen.

EXPERT: They trained us young Sir.

COUNSEL: (To the judge, with a smile.) I have nothing further, Your Honour. . .

My last image of this case was directly following this cross-examination. I walked out of the court and saw the businessman sitting on a seat with his head in his hands. Almost as an apology he shook his head: "I didn't know he was going to say that. I didn't know. . ."

It didn't take the jury long to find a verdict in favour of the journalist.

It only proved what every lawyer will assert in any litigation, "sure things" don't exist.

I'M DOING YOU A FAVOUR!

Herein lies the tale of Ernie, who thought he had outwitted the court system, only to learn that most barristers were not born yesterday.

A small tanker turned into the narrow lane. Ernie Gladesville had been up here, in the dark, many times. Never scraped the old girl yet. The lane was quiet. It was very late, the only activity being shadowed movements cast from the light in the restaurant kitchen above.

Ernie coasted the tanker down the lane's slight incline and braked. The screech could be heard three suburbs away. He instantly dropped his body below windscreen height and waited.

Slowly rising and peering around, Ernie quietly opened the door, walked up to the corner and looked into the cross street. Satisfied, he jogged back to the truck and whipped the two-inch hose from the side. He clamped one end to a tap on the tanker. The other end was dropped into a small hole in a drainage grill in the road. Then he turned a valve at the back of the truck and heard the waste pouring.

Constable Peter Mackiljoy had driven up the street at least seven times that night. Bucks' nights, twenty-firsts and endless celebrations were the cause of more complaints than anything else. He was bored and decided to break routine. Who knows. Maybe he'd stumble onto something more interesting. He turned his patrol car into a sidestreet, eyeing each house on both sides as he went.

What was that?

He braked, and reversed the car back up until it was level with the lane. All he had seen was the tiny red light moving about. There! Some bloke standing in the lane with a cigarette.

The constable got out of the car. As he walked closer, the truck came into view. It had been completely masked by the building's shadow.

MACKILJOY: What are you doing here, Sir?

ERNIE: (Nearly jumping over the truck in fright.) Nothing. Nothing at all. Just resting on this. . . er. . . hose.

The constable walked around behind Ernie and saw the pipe leading into the drain.

MACKILJOY: 'Allo, 'allo, 'allo? What's all this then? *(He had always wanted to say that.)*

ERNIE: That? Well that's just a pipe. I'm just doing my job.

MACKILJOY: Where have you been tonight, Sir?

ERNIE: (Taking a nonchalant puff of the cigarette.) I collect industrial and navy bilge waste. I've been working all night collecting bilge water from the HMAS WOLLONGONG.

MACKILJOY: And pumping it into here, Sir?

Ernie tried to nonchalantly laugh off the suggestion. The copper wasn't convinced. Ernie was arrested.

Things did not go too well for Ernie. His timing was unfortunate. Only a week before his charging, the government had announced tough new laws aimed at combating the scourge of the suburban polluter. A new Act was being enforced. Fines were up. Examples were being made.

Ernie ended up in the Supreme Court before Justice Phyllis Barton, a former politician to whom the events of court were somewhat more enjoyable than her ten years of parliamentary title fights. In court the learned judge felt more like an interested referee, watching the other people knock themselves silly. She only needed to check the clinches once in a while.

The prosecutor opened eloquently. He said the case was clear. The evidence would show that Mr Gladesville siphoned bilge water from the naval ship. Three jars with various types of fuzzy matter were shown to the judge. The first jar, the prosecutor said, was from the defendant's tanker. By comparison with the other samples, it was easy for the judge to conclude that the water found in the drain was actually from the naval ship via the Gladesville truck.

The defence barrister asked to be shown the samples before they were tendered into evidence. He and his solicitor formed an immediate huddle around the subject jar, pointing to various elements within the water and sludge and talking earnestly. Then finally:

"No objection, Your Honour."

With a grimace, Justice Barton watched her associate place the jars on her bench. Keeping some distance, the judge peered through the glass into the murky waters. She pushed each one away with the rubber end of her pencil.

Ernie was sitting behind his solicitor dressed in brown slacks, a short-sleeved shirt and a tie from another era. He shook his head as the allegations were made. Now the crunch.

> *PROSECUTOR:* We allege, Your Honour, that the defendant deliberately, maliciously, pumped this bilge water directly into a suburban drain, to save himself the cost and effort of disposing of the waste legally.

With a sweep of his robe, the prosecutor sat down.

Later it was time for Ernie to give his defence. He was led to the witness stand where, on the instructions of the sheriff's officer, he stood facing the judge, and recited his oath.

Justice Barton had been waiting for this. Over dinner the night before she had pondered what kind of defence the bilge extractor would attempt.

In answer to strategically placed questions from his own counsel, Ernie denied pumping any water into the drain. In fact, said Ernie, he had been sucking water out of the drain. Into his truck. He was clearing the drain. Ernie's barrister warmed to his duty and feigned the role of adversarial inquisitor.

> *ERNIE'S BARRISTER:* So you are telling the court that you were doing a *public service* at the time the police officer saw you?
>
> *ERNIE:* Public service. Yes. That's me. Yes. I was.
>
> *ERNIE'S BARRISTER:* Really?
>
> *ERNIE: (Taking the obvious pass.)* Fair Dinkum! I orta be commended!

With a look of admiration at Ernie, the barrister resumed his seat. Justice Barton looked at the prosecutor. Novel defence. Ernie puffed up his chest. He was too smart for 'em. The prosecutor jumped up, banging his knee on the edge of the bar table but without feeling it.

> *PROSECUTOR:* Mr Gladesville, how much water did you pump from the ship?
>
> *ERNIE:* I filled my tanker.
>
> *PROSECUTOR:* Well then, Mr Gladesville, why was your tanker almost empty when the officer found you?

Silence.

PROSECUTOR: Where did you pump it out, Mr Gladesville?

Silence.

Justice Barton leaned forward and looked at Ernie, and then at Ernie's barrister, who had his head down, looking in a concentrated manner at a crack in the bar table. The tough new anti-pollution laws had just claimed their first quarry.

HE'S GOT THE HEALTH DEPARTMENT BLUES

If you are one of those people who assumes food shops are always clean, then a day in the courts could undermine your sense of security. Take the case of the Bankstown butcher. . .

It was a Thursday afternoon – the busy period. The shop was in the centre of Bankstown, and the restaurants nearby were getting prepared for the weekend business. The shop was crowded. There was no opportunity for the owner, Kerry Richard, to prepare it for the health inspector, due to visit that afternoon. So Kerry quickly checked the freezer, the cutting room and the shop itself. All seemed dirt-free. No sign of any unwanted livestock. The floors were as clean as could be reasonably expected. He'd pass.

The Health Department officer was a little late, and seemed in a hurry. He retraced the steps taken by Kerry earlier in the day. All seemed in order.

Then the man looked behind the display cabinet. Kerry had forgotten about this area. Fearing the worst, he chatted on about business, trying to distract the inspector from looking too closely. To the proprietor's surprise, the man looked up and said the area was fine.

The inspector was facing Kerry and writing his findings on his clipboard. Something then caught Kerry's eye. Movement of some kind.

A black dot on the wall! Please let it be a moth. Please.

Slowly moving his head, to avoid alerting the scribbling officer, Kerry looked at the dot. It was a cockroach. It must have emerged from behind the cutting board.

Kerry knew what this meant. The bugs had moved from their usual residence to the board. That was why it was so clean behind the freezer. Kerry moved into the line of sight of the inspector, who was still unaware that they had company.

The inspector finished his report, handed it to Kerry for countersignature and walked towards the shop door. Kerry took it while continuing to manoeuvre himself to keep the cockroach out of sight. Unfortunately, Kerry had his back to the insect, who had inconveniently decided to move itself further up the wall.

Kerry knew it was all over when the inspector snatched the clipboard back from him. Kerry's attention was drawn to the offending animal. The response was a quick defence.

"Oh. I can explain that. You see we just had the exterminator in. So there will still be one or two cockroaches around. In fact the chemicals will make the cockroaches show up."

The inspector went over to where the bug had been, and he removed a plate on the wall.

He later told the magistrate what he saw: "German cockroaches in all stages of development, too numerous to count, all over the wall. One of the worst cases I've ever seen".

The case seemed clear, but the magistrate thought it was appropriate the owner be called to give his version of events.

MAGISTRATE: Did you say there were only one or two cockroaches?

KERRY: It looked like one or two. But I can explain that.

MAGISTRATE: Did you say the shop had just been visited by a pest person?

KERRY: Yes, and that was why the cockroaches were there. For a couple of days after the extermination, the chemicals bring the survivors out.

INSPECTOR: (Interrupting.) Your worship, we have a receipt by the pest control company. It shows the last extermination was six months before my visit.

MAGISTRATE: (To the butcher.) What do you have to say to that?

KERRY: Time goes fast in a busy shop.

MAGISTRATE: Even so, the premises were quite badly infested.

KERRY: Well, the weather was very hot at the time. . .

INSPECTOR: (Interrupting.) It was July, Your Worship.

At this stage the magistrate asked for Kerry Richard's previous court record.

MAGISTRATE: (After some perusal.) I see you have a conviction recorded over an offence regarding some flies.

KERRY: I can explain that. You see, on that day the front door was propped open. We don't prop the door open any more. We are aware that it lets the flies in. Anyway, that time, the flies saw the door was open and they just thought. . .

The magistrate fined Kerry two thousand dollars.

PS I drove past that butcher shop a few days later. The door was propped open.

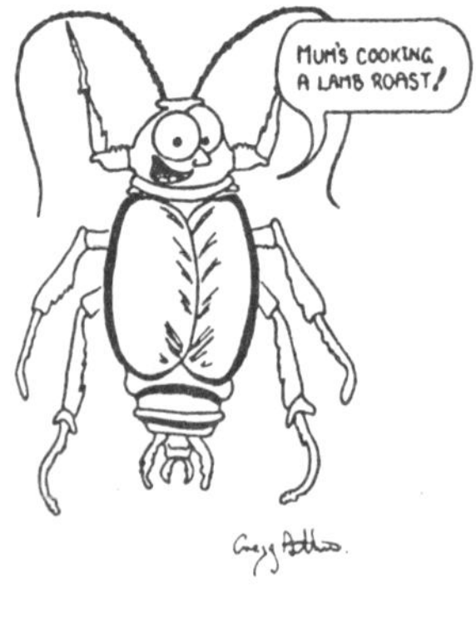

THEY GEE'D ME UP

This really is a true story. It was one of those cases where, despite the seriousness of the offence, you still couldn't help but feel sorry for the guy.

This man had style. He stood at the microphone in the petty sessions courtroom, obviously embarrassed by the situation.

His clothes were immaculate. The shoes had to be worth hundreds. The suit was the type you would never wear for fear of damaging it.

Colour co-ordination – perfect.

Hair – couldn't be better.

This person had style and money – and plenty of both.

As I said, he was embarrassed to be fronting a magistrate and to have his personal details paraded before a packed courtroom.

He had good reason to be embarrassed. This man, Laurence, a chartered accountant, was with two colleagues Michael and Ramone, at a very exclusive city bar late on Friday night.

As is usual in exclusive rooms of this sort, eyes scan and sexual games begin. Laurence was soon in conversation with four of the most beautiful women he had ever seen.

Despite his pedigree and usually excessive self-confidence, Laurence could not believe he was the focus of the women's attention.

Then Michael – probably through envy – starts to brag about some of his own clients, who were well-known businesspeople. The women are distracted away from Laurence.

Then Ramone, accountant to the stars, reveals his impressive clientele. Laurence is by now the forgotten bloke in the white suit sitting by the window. The scene calls for emergency tactics.

> *LAURENCE:* I hope my Porsche convertible will be okay in the driveway.

Bingo. The women's eyes turn to him.

> *LAURENCE:* That's mine out there. The management like me to park it in the driveway. Gives the place class...
>
> *WOMAN A:* I love Porsche convertibles.
>
> *WOMAN B:* I love rides in Porsche convertibles.
>
> *WOMAN C:* I'd love a ride in a Porsche convertible right now.

With this the fourth woman grabs Laurence by the arm. The others aid the general movement towards the door. Laurence resists. He has drunk too much Campari. He had been intending to leave the car overnight. The management didn't mind. Besides Laurence only lived half a kilometre away in a city apartment.

But the women are already in the car and tugging on his coat jacket. They are beautiful. Nah... Laurence won't get caught by the police. What's the chance of a booze bus within half-a-kilometre. Never seen one in this part of the city. We have to pass the cop shop but it'll be fine...

A hundred metres. Sixty kilometres-an-hour already. The women love the car. They're laughing and egging Laurence to go faster. He keeps within the limit.

Two hundred metres. The women are singing "The Road to Gundagai". Loudly.

Three hundred metres. The police station is on the left. A prison van is out the front. No problem. Probably just inside having a Friday night drink with the cops.

Four hundred metres. Laurence is pulled up. He is tested for alcohol. He fails. Laurence is arrested and taken back to the station in the prison van.

The women have disappeared.

The next day, in court. . .

The magistrate asks the police witness why they decided to stop the white Porsche.

CONSTABLE: Well, we were just about to go into the police station to have our Friday night drin. . . discussion, with the local officers when we hear an almighty noise coming from a passing car. We saw a collection of females singing very loudly. We decided to check the state of the driver.

MAGISTRATE: Was he driving erratically?

CONSTABLE: No. Except for the boisterous passengers, all seemed well.

Laurence told the magistrate how he had no intention of driving, and said he was just "gee'd up" by the four beautiful women.

Not a good excuse. Laurence was disqualified from driving for three months and given a large fine.

He went to the bar every Friday for several weeks after the case. He wanted to thank the women for encouraging him to ignore his better judgment, for their police-attracting singing, and for causing him to have his first conviction.

But he never saw them again.

Such is life in the fast lane. . .

THE CHEQUERED LADY

Frauds, whether they are tax evasion or the comparatively small amounts involved in social security frauds, are often committed by people who are decent citizens in all other respects. Sometimes the defrauders come to believe they have a right *to their ill-gotten gains, even after they have been found guilty in a court. And usually it's not arrogance – they honestly believe they've been wrongly treated.*

Being at the counter of the Woolgambogook Social Security office, Errol had to deal with some desperate people: needy mothers complaining about cheques not arriving on time; underpayment complaints. . .

Few of Errol's customers were particularly happy people. Usually he could handle the situation but today's woman was a real worry. And it was all over a late cheque. The woman had demanded instant reimbursement. She claimed she couldn't pay her rent. She claimed she was being threatened with eviction. She, in turn, threatened Errol.

The woman was aged in her late seventies. Errol knew that if she did complain he could have a difficult time with the bleeding heart supervisors.

Errol felt he had to say something. The woman had been so abusive and threatening that he feared what action his superiors would take if he didn't get in first. Errol rang his immediate supervisor and asked for an appointment.

Two hours later he was relating the events of the morning to the supervisor, Kath. She asked him all the routine questions – had he been rude first? Had he retaliated? What had he told the woman about the late cheque? By the end of the meeting Kath was satisfied Errol had acted properly in dealing with the client. She asked him to print out a copy of the woman's file. She also wanted Errol to check the address – just to make sure the cheque didn't go to the wrong place.

Late that afternoon Errol knocked on Kath's door. He entered room with a long printout in his hands. He closed the door after him.

Errol told Kath he had carried out the check on the woman's file – it was true that she received the age pension. Errol then dropped the bombshell:

ERROL: I checked the address. This address has seven pension cheques sent to it under different names. . .

KATH: (Not particularly impressed.) Well obviously there are seven people living there who are in receipt of pensions from our department.

ERROL: I checked that too. It's a two-bedroom cottage. The woman also claimed she lived alone.

KATH: It could be a mailing address for the other. . .

ERROL: I also checked with Veteran's Affairs. They told me that they also send two cheques to that address – under another two names. It'd be a pretty busy mailing address.

KATH: All right, all right. How long have these cheques been going to this one house.

Dramatic pause.

ERROL: Twenty-two years.

Shocked pause.

ERROL: (Continuing.) I figure she is picking up about three thousand bucks a fortnight. . . and she has the gall to attack me over a late cheque!

An official investigation was started that afternoon. Errol had been right. From 1970, the woman had been receiving ten cheques under false names. For some unknown reason, she dropped one of the names in 1981, and continued taking the money for the other nine false claims. During the twenty-two years, the woman had bought ten properties. She had received more than half-a-million dollars from the two departments in excess of her proper entitlement. She had also been able to successfully apply for a rent allowance. Investigations showed she owned the property she was living in. The department was giving her rent to pay to herself.

The court was told the case was the most serious social security fraud in Australia's history – not only in terms of the money taken – but also in the number of false names used.

When deciding what to do with the woman, the judge asked if she had any criminal record. When asking this question, he really expected to be told the elderly, matronly woman's record was clean.

The truth was quite different.

In 1963 she had been convicted of forging a will and a mortgage document.

In 1971 she was again convicted of forgery and uttering. She was jailed for eighteen months.

It seems she was receiving the ten false benefits while she was serving time for the 1971 offences.

Despite the woman's age, the judge said he had no alternative but to jail her for a minimum of two years.

The judge also remarked that it was interesting that the woman used the same address for all the false names for twenty-two years, but neither department had detected the problem.

PS The woman was ordered to pay the money back – which she did. But because the frauds went back so many years, the interest she was forced to pay out was phenomenal. In all she was ordered to repay 1.2 million dollars. She had to sell all the properties she bought with the fraud money. In fact the woman became a bankrupt.

One ponders how long the scam would have lasted if the woman hadn't complained about the late cheque. . .

I CAN EXPLAIN THAT!

It has often been said that one can never overestimate the cunning ability of the criminal mind. As any detective will attest, the experienced crims have a prodigious ability to "think on their feet" during a police interview. This is a case about a man who thought he knew all the answers.

Larry followed the detective into the interview room and sat at the chair next to the table. His nerves, quite calm up until now, started to get edgy. The whole experience had been very traumatic. The detective had come into the pub, and gruffly asked Larry to accompany him down to the station. The detective said he wanted to question Larry about his allegation that he had been robbed.

Larry had been operating the betting agency the night before, and he claimed that a group of masked men forced him to place heavy bets – without giving him any of the bet money. According to Larry the masked men took the winnings for these bets as they were released by the computer.

The detective sat Larry down in one of the interview rooms and asked him if he would like a cup of coffee. Coffee dispensed, the officer got to the point:

> *DETECTIVE:* Sir, just to check. You were on duty last night at the Clarence Arms Hotel at approximately ten?
>
> *LARRY: (Taking a sip.)* Yes I was. It started as a quiet night. No Trouble. At the beginning everything was going smoothly. Smooth as silk.
>
> *DETECTIVE:* Right. And you were operating the hotel-based betting system last night.

LARRY: Yes. There were two trots meetings on. Not a lot of interest in that around here. Some people came in and had bets, but not many.

DETECTIVE: Now can you tell me about these masked gunmen?

LARRY: Oh yes. I'll never forget them. . .

He then told how three men had lounged around at the back of the agency for about an hour, obviously waiting for the punters to leave. When asked what the three men looked like, Larry said they never looked at him directly in the face, so he couldn't describe them. Besides when the agency emptied, they put on the balaclavas and pulled out shortened firearms.

Larry said these men made him place the false bets between nine and eleven o'clock.

The detective asked Larry if he was sure about the time.

Larry was sure.

The detective threw his pen down:

DETECTIVE: Sir, an inspector from the agency's central office came into the your building at ten o'clock. The office was concerned about the large bets being placed on such a quiet night. In fact, he said the bets were so large that they were equal to the size of bets one would receive on Melbourne Cup day. As was usual for spot checks, the inspector was wearing ordinary street clothes.

Sir, this inspector told us this morning that he saw nothing out of the ordinary. No gunmen. No balaclavas.

LARRY: (Raging defensively.) Of course he wouldn't see anything. When anyone came near the agency a fourth bloke out the front warned the others, and they all went to hide.

DETECTIVE: Sir, the agency you operated is only one room. Where could anybody hide?

LARRY: (Sarcastically.) Where else? The toilet of course. We do have toilets – even in the little agencies.

DETECTIVE: I think I should inform you that the inspector says he came into the shop, saw you and no-one else, stayed around for a few minutes and then went into the toilet to wait for while. He saw no masked gunmen in the toilet. Heard no noises. Nothing. How do you explain that?

LARRY: I can explain that. I saw that the men all went into the women's toilet. They obviously thought there wouldn't be any women interested in trots meetings.

DETECTIVE: Sir, the inspector hid in the women's toilets, not the men's. He saw there were no women in the agency, so he knew he could stay in the ladies' for a while and listen for anything unusual. Now to repeat, he said he saw nothing. Can you explain that?

Larry couldn't believe it. Bad timing and an unluckily shrewd inspector had blown the perfect fraud. His masked gunmen story had failed him.

Guilty pleas were entered. Larry took it philosophically. . . and thought over his mistakes.

Next time he would say the robbers went into the men's toilets.

THE BOGUS DOCTOR

This is the amazing story of Doctor Lynette May Simpton, a woman who ran consulting rooms, performed surgery and prescribed drugs at her busy practice. . . but all was not what it seemed.

Jim Stambouki lay on the padded table in the surgery. The surgery assistant said the doctor would only be a minute.

A short time later a white-gowned heavily set woman opened the door and introduced herself as Doctor Simpton and shook his aching hand. Jim told the doctor about the accident at the worksite. He had been putting up scaffolding for the painters at Tullamarine airport. The carriage had suddenly become unstable and Jim had slipped. He had grabbed onto the edge of the plywood platform and saved himself from a four-metre fall, but in the process a four-inch splinter had caught in his forearm. The supervisor had told him to go home and get the local GP to fix it up.

Doctor Simpton looked very closely at the injury. This would require some delicate work.

Jim felt sick. The thought of going under the knife terrified him. He was not a good patient.

Doctor Simpton called in her assistant and asked for a dose of local anaesthetic to be prepared.

The operation was a difficult one – the wood kept breaking. But after an hour or so all the pieces were out. Jim was told a take two days off, change the dressings every evening and come back the next week. He was asked to settle the account with the receptionist outside.

The injured man gingerly replaced his jacket, and walked out into the waiting room.

There were two serious-looking women standing at the counter. The receptionist was nonplussed:

> *RECEPTIONIST:* I'm sorry, she is very busy. You'll just have to wait.
> *WOMAN ONE:* No. *I'm* sorry my good woman. We *will* see her now.
> *WOMAN TWO:* Do we need to break into the surgery?

Jim, growing concerned by the women's threatening attitude, asked them to settle down. He told them the doctor was just cleaning up after an operation.

> *WOMAN ONE:* Doctor? She's not a doctor. She's not even a qualified chemist. She's just pretending to be a doctor. We're from the Health Department.
> *WOMAN TWO:* I pity anyone who comes under *her* knife.

Jim fainted.

Some months later.

Jim sat outside the Magistrate's Court while the two women from the Health Department entered. They were followed by Doctor Simpton, who was accompanied by a woman in a grey suit and carrying a barrister's blue bag.

After half an hour, Jim was called to give evidence. He told the magistrate about the events at the worksite and in the surgery. . . including the fainting.

The woman in the grey suit – the doctor's counsel – stood to cross-examine Jim:

> *BARRISTER:* Mr Stambouki, did this woman, at any time, say she was a doctor?
> *JIM:* Yes.
> *BARRISTER:* Are you sure about that?

JIM: Yes.

BARRISTER: Is it possible you are mistaken? Just possible?

JIM: It's possible but. . .

BARRISTER: Thank you.

Jim was upset. He knew the woman said she was doctor, but he thought that by admitting the possibility of error, he might have blown the case.

He needn't have worried. The Health Department had other evidence:

WOMAN ONE: So, after receiving this tip-off, we check the records. There is no medical registration card for a Lynette Simpton. We go to the alleged surgery and see a shingle hanging out the front door. It reads:

DOCTOR LYNETTE SIMPTON
BACHELOR OF MEDICINE
BACHELOR OF SURGERY MBBS PHD OA

We enter the surgery where, while we demand to see Ms Simpton, Mr Stambouki faints.

Jim bows his head in embarrassment, knowing the whole court is now looking at him.

WOMAN ONE: The self-called doctor comes out. We ask her if she has been putting herself up as a doctor. She answers "No. Of course not. Don't be ridiculous". We ask about the shingle out the front. She says "What shingle?" We all go to look and it's not there.

Ms Simpton gets huffy and threatens to sue the Health Department for disturbing her "counselling practice".

We decide to leave and carry out further investigations. We make sure we get Mr Stambouki's phone number.

The next day we return. The shingle is back out the front. We have it photographed, and we enter the premises again. Once more we demand to see Ms Simpton. And again she threatens us. And again we go outside and there is no shingle. But this time we have the photograph, which proves she is advertising herself as a doctor. With the evidence of Mr Stambouki, we decide to launch a prosecution.

The doctor is called to the stand, and is questioned by her own counsel:

BARRISTER: Is there a shingle?

SIMPTON: Yes.

BARRISTER: Where did it come from?

SIMPTON: Well. . . I always wanted to be a doctor. Right from the time I was a little girl. But I could never pass the exams. I just had no aptitude for learning. . .

Jim's arm started to throb.

SIMPTON: My family saved up and bought me the shingle. Just to make me feel better, I guess.

After all, I wasn't able to get into Uni. So I worked as a cleaner.

Jim's arm was hurting a lot.

BARRISTER: What experience did you acquire?

SIMPTON: Hardly any.

BARRISTER: How many operations did you perform as a non-qualified person.

SIMPTON: (Very proudly.) Mr Stambouki was my first. It worked out pretty well I think. I just winged it!

After being told that this case was the most flagrant breach of the Act, the magistrate fined "Dr" Simpton substantially, and warned her that any repetition of this conduct would result in a jail sentence.

Jim missed the sentencing. He was being given smelling salts in the prosecutor's room down the hall.

BIKIES? WHAT BIKIES?

This was a case of a complete, comprehensive demolition of what was almost the perfect defence.

Jack was an unassuming man. There he stood, in the middle of the court, in his safari suit, hearing the serious charges against him being outlined.

> *PROSECUTOR:* Your Worship, in addition to the two hundred gun licence charges, there are eleven counts of possessing illegal firearms, one of possessing a shortened weapon. . .

Jack shook his head. The whole case was preposterous.

> *PROSECUTOR:* And we allege bikie gangs were involved, Your Worship. We allege this man bought these weapons for the purpose of selling them to local bikie gangs. . . and the Mafia. The Mafia too, Your Worship.

Jack sniggered indignation. But it was soon time for him to explain why 241 guns were found in his modest suburban home.

Jack told the magistrate the whole problem arose because he cared too much for his fellow man. He said he had been approached by a man who wanted weapons to be used to fight Soviet soldiers who had invaded Czechoslovakia. Joe outlined some of his own history, saying he had dealt first-hand with the communists in the Second World War. Communism was evil, he said. It was worse than "Hitlerism", he said. It was his duty to fight the scourge.

No, the guns were not for the Mafia or bikie gangs. Anyway, what bikie gangs? Joe said he had never met a bikie in his life. No sir, no weapons for bikies.

Just before he left the stand, Jack added he did not receive any profit from the purchase and sale of the mercenary weapons. It was an act involving morality of the highest degree. Jack then strutted out of the stand, and took a seat next to his equally indignant wife.

The magistrate's eyes followed Jack back to the floor of the court.

> *MAGISTRATE:* The accused says he sent the weapons overseas. There is no record of this. The accused says the weapons were to help fight the communists in Czechoslovakia. Well, I know for a personal fact that the Soviets moved *out* of that country at least a year before the guns were bought.

Jack did not change his dignified expression.

> *MAGISTRATE:* Now for the accused's claim that he did not know any bikies. . .

The magistrate shuffled his papers:

> *MAGISTRATE:* Ah yes. The lighter. The accused claims he did not know any bikies. If this is the case, then how does he explain this cigarette lighter found in his house on the day of the raid. It is a gold lighter with the inscription: "To Jack, from the Hell's Angels".

Jack remained dignified, but his solicitor started doodling. He had given it his best shot. Better luck next time.

> *MAGISTRATE:* Or how could the accused explain the two bikies who rode up to his house while plain clothes police were searching it. The two motorcyclists, obviously unaware that the searchers were police officers, asked if Jack was around. They asked if Jack had their guns ready yet.

The magistrate grappled with other pieces of paper:

> *MAGISTRATE:* And what about the crossbows, submachine guns, 174 rifle barrels, assorted bolts, converted replica pistols, starting guns. . .

Jack hung his head. It was over. But not for the magistrate:

> *MAGISTRATE:* And your bank accounts. Deposits of $3000; $2500 and $2200 into one account in the same month, followed by another $2000 eight weeks later, and $2400 a week after that. . .

The magistrate took another fifteen minutes to outline the evidence against Jack, including affidavits from interstate gun dealers that Jack had bought up to another 200 guns which were never found.

In the end Jack was jailed for eighteen months. He was relieved. The way the magistrate was going, Jack was starting to wonder whether capital punishment was a possibility.

YOU SIMPLY *MUST* PLACE AN AD WITH US!

This case is proof that some criminals will go to extraordinary lengths to earn a dishonest dollar.

Julie sighed when she saw the pile of bills for the shop. The fish man, potatoes, electricity, water, gas. . . This was going to take at least an hour.

She almost discarded the letter from Welsh Publishing as junk mail, when she noticed the letter had a bill-type window on the front.

Impatiently she ripped the front, expecting the mail to be simply a clever junk ploy.

It read:

Dear Mr Stambouka,

Please find enclosed the invoice for the advertisements run in the "Tree and Bush Weekly", "The Jogger" and "The Clarinet and Bassoon Monthly Journal". Also please find attached complimentary copies of the magazines.

We would appreciate your prompt payment of the account. If this is not done within seven (7) days, we will be forced to charge interest on the outstanding amount at twenty-five (25) percent per annum.

Yours,

Gareth Owen Edwards

Julie stomped furiously into the shop.

"Tony! Didn't I say we didn't need any advertising! Didn't I? Didn't I?"

Tony was stopped in the process of straining some potato scallops. Both he and the customer looked in fright at the enraged woman.

"Well Tony? Why did you place the ads when we decided we couldn't afford them?"

Tony almost began to blurt out some feeble defence, when he realised he hadn't placed any ads.

Julie showed her husband the bill. He returned to the scallops. It was a mistake, that's all.

The woman checked the magazines that came with the bill and found there were ads for their shop. Tony saw the ads and laughed.

"Well they haven't improved business. Ay, they've even got a little drawing of the shop, with me in the window. I'm going to get it framed."

Julie was going to Consumer Affairs.

Meanwhile, at a physiotherapist's office in the city. . .

The receptionist broke the sticky tape seal with her small fingernail. She pulled out the magazine, titled "Tree Surgery For All Ages".

The woman quickly flipped over the envelope, to check the mail was not wrongly delivered. Why would such a boring magazine be delivered to a physiotherapist's office?

She pulled out the covering letter and invoice.

Funny. . . why would the boss put an ad in a magazine? The practice was booked up for months ahead.

Meanwhile, in a suburban workshop. . .

"I tell you, I didn't place any ad in no bloody magazine", Stan was getting annoyed. He was repairing a Hoover 125 washer. These things didn't leave much room to work inside.

Stan emerged from under the contraption. He was a balding rotund man, in his fiftieth year as a "fix-it" man.

He wiped his hands on his overalls and took the invoice from his wife. He read the letter, put his glasses on, and read it again.

"Well, they're not gettin' any money outta me for some ads I never asked for. I'm tellin' you this for a start off!"

The ad scam annoyed the magistrate. He was also annoyed because the person who sent the letters was unknown.

In the six months since Tony and Julie, Stan and the physiotherapist made their complaints, John Gunner and his staff from Consumer Affairs had tried every possible way to catch the newspaper rorters.

> *JOHN GUNNER:* No, Your Worship. Although we have the companies responsible, it appears the people behind the false ads have covered themselves so well that they are difficult to touch.

Stan elbowed the well-dressed young man who happened to be sitting next to him in the back of the court:

> *STAN:* I wish I knew who they were. I'd touch 'em!
> *STAN'S WIFE:* Shut up. You're in a courtroom.

Magistrate Jack Hearey asked to see the magazines, and spent some minutes perusing them closely.

> *MAGISTRATE:* What is the circulation of these magazines?
> *JOHN GUNNER:* None, Your Worship.
> *MAGISTRATE:* None?
> *JOHN GUNNER:* None.
> *MAGISTRATE:* Why? They don't look all that bad. For instance there's a lovely article on preventing woodrot in a Canadian Cypress. . .

JOHN GUNNER: No, Your Worship. They were only made up for the people who were being duped. It's an old practice called "blowing". Although in this case it appears the perpetrators went to a lot of trouble and expense just for the false revenue. There are only three or four of each magazine printed.

The magistrate frowned. He had been intending to subscribe.

MAGISTRATE: All right then. If it was in my power, the people behind this scam would be behind bars. But since we don't know who they are I can't do it. However, I can make it sting a little. I fine the company which printed the magazines fifty thousand dollars. Also, did anyone actually pay any money to the company?

JOHN GUNNER: (Smiling.) Well no, Your Worship. It seemed that all the intended. . . how should I say. . . dupees. . . came straight to my department.

MAGISTRATE: So the company didn't make a brass razoo?

JOHN GUNNER: Not a zac.

Stan laughed loudly, and his wife hit him with her newspaper. The magistrate shifted the papers over to the "out" tray.

STAN: (Calling out.) Crime doesn't pay. Ay, Mag?

The magistrate looked up at the overalled man and smiled.

MAGISTRATE: Yes, there are less expensive ways of earning a living.

STAN: One other thing, Mag, what's a dupee?

STAN'S WIFE: You wear one of them on your head.

The court broke into laughter, and Stan left the courtroom without saying another word. . .

I'M NOT A CRIMINAL!

Who would you expect to get public support: (a) an offender? or (b) the arresting officer? Read on. The answer might surprise you.

A sunny day in the city.

Lunchtime.

Joanne Zerbos was half running along the city street. She had taken too long to choose the skirt. By the time she had eaten lunch, chatted to her boyfriend on the shopping-centre phone, and tried on all the pieces in the boutique, her forty-five minutes had skipped away.

She was late and the boss at the restaurant would not understand. Again.

Detective Sergeant Ted Smith was also late. He'd had a stroll around the city.

Ted was due to appear as a witness in a city court. This was a rare change. Most days Ted was stuck in the same suburban station where he had been assigned for the past ten years.

Joanne calculates. If she can keep this pace up, she might be able to get to the restaurant only ten minutes late. She'd be able to sneak in, throw on the apron and start mingling with the patrons. She might fool the boss. He probably wouldn't give her another chance. This is the third late lunch this week. And it's only Wednesday.

Oh no. Wouldn't you know it. It was just Joanne's luck that a bunch of schoolkids had spread themselves right across the footpath. Excursions ought to be banned. What about us hard-working types? How are we supposed to get to our jobs and keep the country running?

Get out of the way, you brats.

"'Scuse me mate."

Ted was politely shuffled to the side by a shiny-suited young man in a hurry. Ted scowled at the back of the passer-by.

Look at him. Never done a decent day's work in his life. Never got time for anybody, that type. Probably a corporate crim.

Joanne could see the restaurant down the bottom of the hill. At least the boss wasn't out the front looking up and down for her like the last time.

Oh no. Not these bloody lights.

Every afternoon Joanne plays mind games with the lights. Every afternoon she loses. Not once in the three months she had been working at the restaurant had she caught the green "walk" light. Not once. It was always red. And they are the slowest set of lights in the city. The traffic turns right on arrows from three directions – an extra lane turning left with its own set of lights, and a usual bank-up of traffic on all sides. Strange how they can put a man on the moon, but they can't. . .

Ted's stroll had turned into a brisk walk – not so much from the wish to avoid the magistrate's wrath, as from the frustration of being pushed aside by the shiny suit. The twerp.

He approaches the corner and waits with the rest of the pedestrians.

He's anxious now. The lights are taking a long time.

Just then he sees a woman break out of the group and charge across the road against the "Don't Walk" sign.

Normally Ted wouldn't care. But this is a bit brazen. All thoughts of his own pressing appointment suddenly vanish. He'd better say something.

"Hey you!"

Joanne hears the voice behind her. It couldn't be for her. The sign is red, but who pays attention to the lights?

She keeps walking.

The "Hey you!" is repeated, only this time it is louder and a bit scary.

All right, he means me. But I'm not stopping. If he's that serious he can come after me. But he won't.

Joanne's arm is grabbed, and she is spun around to see a pair of angry eyes.

"Stop when I call you, my young woman. I'm a police officer."

Joanne instantly considered her options: fright, flight or fight. She chooses the latter.

"Assault! Help! This man is assaulting me!"

The bulky man before her becomes official: "Tell me your name".

"I'm not telling. Assault!"

"Well then you're coming with me."

"Oh yeah. Okay funny man. What's this? Candid camera? Where's Alan Funt?"

Ted pushes the woman back onto the footpath. Decisive action needed here. Should he warn her and let her go? Okay. He doesn't want to be stuck with her. Ted starts issuing a warning, but the fool woman keeps yelling and starts claiming police brutality. If he lets her go, there could be a complaint in it. At least if he takes her in he could put his side first.

Ted leads the struggling woman up the street, looking for a station where he can charge her with jay walking.

Unfortunately, Ted is not familiar with the city, and although police headquarters is only a hundred metres away, the good Sergeant is unaware of this fact.

Instead, he leads his charge up two blocks, asking if anyone has seen a police station nearby – but the Sydneysiders are not very helpful. Funny that *nobody* knows where there's a police station.

The search continues.

And continues.

Eventually a station is found and Ted lays his charge against Joanne. Joanne, who is now tired and thirsty, as well as upset, is offered a drink by a woman constable in the station but she replies that she'd rather lay a charge against Ted.

Two hours later Joanne returns to work, only to be fired by an unsympathetic boss.

Some weeks later Joanne appears in court. A magistrate hears the police version of events and, without raising an eyebrow, convicts Joanne under the *General Traffic Regulations* 1937 and fines her twenty dollars. She is ordered to pay another forty-five dollars for the court's time.

Joane was on the front page of the tabloids the next day, holding up the court notice, and looking very sorry for herself.

I've never forgotten the words my colleague uttered when he was finally convinced that the story was true:

"It's good to know they're out there protecting us, eh?"

ALL IN *HIS* NAME

One of the more entertaining aspects of watching court cases is the excuse *– the alleged reasons offered by people desperately trying to avoid jail. In this case, the reason was genuine, the logic incomprehensible.*

Gerry was at the counter of his music shop, phone in each ear, trying to sort out suppliers when a set of fingernails tapped on the glass in front of him.

Gerry looked up to see a willowy, slightly anaemic and academic-looking man demanding attention.

The rather rude man said he wanted to buy $20,000 worth of musical equipment – now.

Gerry hung up both phones.

Two hours later a range of instruments had been selected, including three tubas, a mobile organ, a double bass, a range of woodwind and several dozen maracas.

Gerry, barely able stop his shaking hand, totalled up the prospective sale. It only came to $19,956.

The willowy man smiled and pointed to the guitar leads on the wall behind the shopowner. These were then also noted down on the invoice.

Having given his name, address and phone number, the man left, saying he would be back in two weeks – on the twenty-first of the month – to pick up the assembled and packed instruments.

That night Gerry took his wife for a champagne dinner at Circular Quay.

The order was assembled, but there was a snag. The trombone wouldn't be there on time. The supplier had made a mistake.

Gerry rang the customer's number. The retirement village had never heard of someone with that name. There must be a mistake with the phone number. Gerry looked up the phone book, but no address matched the surname.

He thought for a moment. There was something else that the man had said. Something about a church. He said he worked at a Darlinghurst church. It was a strange name – All Saints United Episcopal or something.

Eventually Gerry found the number, but again the name was unknown.

Must have been a mistake. No matter. He had a cash-only policy anyway.

On the afternoon of the twenty-first, the willowy man entered the store. Gerry, despite his fears about the man's identification, was still enthusiastic about the sale. He had been able to find a replacement trombone.

The news, however, wasn't good. The man wanted to pay by personal cheque. He was unable to pay cash.

The sale was a huge one, so Gerry said he would take a bank cheque. The man agreed and said he would be back with one later that day.

Gerry looked closely at the bank cheque. There was something wrong with it. He just couldn't pinpoint the problem, but there was something wrong.

The man was smiling at him across the counter, asking if he could start loading the gear into his van outside. Gerry asked him to wait a minute. In the storeroom, a lamp was turned onto the cheque. The figure. There was something wrong with the figure. Gerry called the police.

He slowly walked back into the shop and was greeted by the smiling face:

"Everything all right?"

"Ah Yes. . . I just have to confirm the cheque, that's all. . . "

"But it's a bank cheque!"

"Sure, but I have to check – for my own safety, you know. . ." Gerry sighed relief when the two officers walked in the door. He had only called them two minutes ago.

"Excuse me Sir. Did you ask for assistance?"

The willowy man pretended to read the music magazines through the glass counter.

"Ah yes. I just want to check this cheque." Gerry felt doubt about his actions, and started feeling he had blown a major sale through silly panicking.

One of the officers took the cheque and held it up the light.

Dizzy relief ran through Gerry as the officer pronounced judgment:

"John, there's something wrong here."

The willowy man kept reading magazine covers.

Officer John agreed with the diagnosis and wanted to know the whereabouts of the attempted perpetrator.

At this the willowy man looked up.

"All right. It was me. I doctored the cheque. I went into the bank this morning and got a bank cheque for two dollars ten cents. I then took it home and fiddled it around to the twenty thousand. I needed the instruments for my local church. HE (looking upwards) needed the instruments. So I thought they were first priority. I thought HE would understand. And I think he does. So I came in this morning and tried to get the instruments. They were for HIM, you know."

The officers stared at the man. The senior officer started the usual warning about not having to say anything unless a solicitor was present, but there was no point. The willowy man had given a most complete confession, including motive, in front of a witness. Or witnesses – two Mauritian musicians had postponed their conga-hunting during the confession and had listened, chins on palms on the glass counter.

Gerry was thanked for his diligence, and the man was asked to step out onto the footpath. The shop, complete with orphaned assorted instruments was quiet once more.

The next day Gerry received a call from the police officer. No, he would not be required in court. No, the man stood by his confession. The officer just thought Gerry might like to know that the willowy man listed his occupation as "student" and "part-time minister". The man was indeed a fill-in minister, and was studying theology and philosophy. In fact the forger was in the middle of a thesis on the meaning and operations of the Ten Commandments. . .

THE CASE OF THE SENSITIVE NEW-AGE COPS

Courts and tribunals hear the most extraordinary cases of people acting inappropriately. Usually the motivation is money.

It is the duty of police officers to inform relatives of the deaths of close ones. Sam and his partner Rex hated this part of the job – every officer does.

They had found the man's body on a property not far outside their township.

The dead man's wife had reported him missing; and it wasn't until some weeks had passed that a local resident expressed concern that the man's utility had not left the site where there was a little house, for at least a fortnight.

Rex and Sam went to check on the property and found the man's body in the house. It seemed obvious he had shot himself. Both officers examined the land closely. It was a nice piece of property, but they found no sign of suspicious circumstances. The investigation could be ended quite quickly, but before returning to the station, they just wanted to take one last look at the little house. . .

Finally there remained one job – to inform the dead man's wife of the discovery. Since Sam and Rex had found the body, they were given the unpleasant chore of informing the woman of her husband's fate.

By this time it was quite late, but the decision had been taken at the station that the woman should be informed immediately.

The officers pulled into the woman's driveway. Rex commented that the enormous floodlit house before them was going to require a regular income to maintain.

Sam got out and rang the front doorbell. It was answered by a middle-aged woman in a dressing gown and slippers. Her face told the officers that she had guessed the reason for their visit.

They were invited into the house. Once seated she asked them if they had come with information about her husband. Sam answered in the affirmative and then told her about the circumstances of the death.

The woman had obviously been braced for the news for some time, but even so, broke into tears.

Sam sat while the woman let out some instantaneous grief. Rex then tapped him on the leg and whispered:

> *REX:* Come on. . . let's ask about it now. . .
>
> *SAM:* Now?
>
> *REX:* Yeah, why not? *(And then to the woman.)* Excuse me. . . I. . . err. . . we. . . were just wondering about that property where we found your husband.
>
> *WOMAN: (Through tears.)* Oh yes. I suppose you want some information for your investigation. I really don't know much about the land. Olaf handled all that. . .
>
> *REX: (Interrupting.)* No, no. We were wondering whether you'd be interested in selling. It looks like a nice little property, and I've been looking for a place like that for some time. . .

Rex was stopped by an incredulous stare from the bereaved woman. It told him he had stepped way over the line. Sam stepped in to try to salvage the situation:

> *SAM:* If you don't want to discuss it tonight, we can come back tomorrow. It's just that Rex doesn't want to see the property go to someone else.

The same stare – slightly aggravated – stopped the ambitious Sam.

> *WOMAN:* You come here to tell me my Olaf is dead. You tell a woman she is a widow. And then you try to turn the episode into a real estate transaction. Get out of here. . .

Sam and Rex left. They discussed the ungratefulness of the woman. After all, they had come out in the middle of the night to break the news about a death. What was wrong with offering to remedy her financial position? They shrugged and agreed it had been worth a shot. The property *was* very nice. Besides, she'd cool down by morning.

Two weeks later they were informed the woman had made a complaint to the commissioner. The commissioner had, in turn, referred it to the Police Tribunal for assessment and recommendations.

At the hearing the woman had shown few signs of having cooled down. She told the tribunal she was amazed that the officer wanted to discuss the property during the same visit in which he broke the news of her husband's suicide.

Rex and Sam were eventually chastened by the tribunal, and allowed to go on their way. Right through the hearing, and even as they left, they appeared amazed – amazed at all this kerfuffle over a late-night whim. After all, it *was* a nice piece of property. . .

So much for the sensitive New-Age cop!

WHAT! ME NOT PAY?

It is often said that some people will say anything and promise anything to avoid going to jail. The theory also states that these same people, if reprieved, will just as quickly forget that promise. I have seen many such cases, but none as flagrant as "Mr Caviar".

We had been chasing this guy all over Sydney. The difficulty was not changing addresses or business offices, but rather changing courts. He refused to pay in so many restaurants throughout Sydney, we reporters did not know where he would turn up next.

Bingo. The dock at Waverley Court.

MR CAVIAR: (To magistrate.) Your Worship, I intended to pay for the meal. I am not well. I must eat. My friends will help me pay for the meals. I just cannot locate my friends.

MAGISTRATE: From a look at your record I can see that this is not the first time you have done this.

MR CAVIAR: I do not know what you mean. I have always paid for my meals.

MAGISTRATE: Sergeant, how many prior offences are alleged.

SERGEANT: Fifty-two, Your Worship.

MAGISTRATE: (After a shocked pause.) Fifty-two?

SERGEANT: Fifty-two.

Someone in the public gallery laughed. The accused man in the dock shrugged his shoulders and looked ahead blankly.

The magistrate regained his composure. He was accustomed to the eccentricities of eastern suburbs people. Only last week he had to deal with a man who was making a nuisance of himself by claiming he was the lost Tsarina Anastasia.

MAGISTRATE: Read me the facts alleged in this case please Sergeant.

They went like this. . . On two days within a week the man had entered restaurants in the city and the eastern suburbs. Each time he ordered the meals, ate, ordered wine, drank, then asked for the manager and admitted his parlous financial position. The last time, the manager called the police and the highly satisfied man burped a complete admission. He apologised for the non-payment and was carted off.

MAGISTRATE: (To Mr Caviar.) Are you asking for bail?

MR CAVIAR: Yes, Your Worship. I promise I will not do it again.

MAGISTRATE: All right. Are you able to provide bail money?

MR CAVIAR: Your Highness. . . I cannot find any such money.

SERGEANT: (Under breath.) If he had the money he would've paid for the bloody meals.

MAGISTRATE: But without bail money you cannot be released into the community. It is the only way that we can be sure that you will actually attend court at the next sitting.

MR CAVIAR: But Your Majesty, I can be trusted. I promise you now that I will not do anything like this again.

SERGEANT: (Under breath again.) That makes fifty-three personal guarantees.

Scene: Central Local Court. (Some weeks later.)

RESTAURATEUR: (Obviously still annoyed. Spitting his story to yet another incredulous magistrate.) Then he orders the place out. Appetiser. Entree. Steak. Dessert. Then, he wants the wine list. Why not, we say. He orders a top bottle. Great, we say. And then he goes around to the other tables offering to buy drinks for the other customers. Sure, they say. Why not. It becomes a merry old party. But when the bill comes he says. . . he says. . . *(glaring at the accused man)* he says he can't pay. He said he couldn't even pay for the drinks he bought the other diners.

The accused man is put on the witness stand. What did he have to say about the scandalous allegations?

MR CAVIAR: (With a puffed-out chest and a sweep of the arm.) The steak was the best I have ever had. I recommend the restaurant to anyone.

RESTAURATEUR: Oh joy. Oh joy. Get ready for the rush.

The magistrate wanted the accused man to be psychologically tested.

A few months later the same face popped up in the same court. The tally was up to 54 non-payments.

Again the magistrate was incredulous. Again the man promised not to do it again. Again he couldn't raise bail. Again he recommended the restaurant.

The last I heard he was in jail.

At least he won't have to pay for the food.

DOMESTIC BLISS

This is a tale of Tom Boyle – a most unusual man with an unusually heavy chip on his shoulder, a man who thought justice was permanently on his side. He was in for a surprise.

"Ada. Where the bloody hell are you?", Tom Boyle raged through the house, flinging doors and kicking chairs. He had known as soon as he walked in the front door that Ada had left him. But it made him feel better to whack something.

Boyle slouched in one of the overstuffed lounge chairs.

She said she'd leave. She'd said so many times before, but had never done it. She was very upset after he punched her the night before. But that wouldn't have been enough of a reason to walk out. It must have been her brother Charles in Brisbane who made her go.

Twenty years he had been married to Ada.

Twenty years.

Well, she's coming back, and there's nothing her brother is going to do to stop it.

That night at Charles' home. . .

"Phone for you, Charles."

As Charles approached, Rhonda covered the mouthpiece and whispered, "I think it's Tom Boyle. . . calling from Adelaide".

Charles held the phone for a few moments before raising it to his ear.

CHARLES: Tom, Tom Boyle. Is that you?

TOM: Don't give me any of your "ho ho" friendly 'ellos, mate! Where's my wife?

CHARLES: Settle down, Tom.

TOM: Don't tell me to settle down, you pillock.

CHARLES: Look Tom. I know where she is. But mate, she doesn't want to see you.

TOM: (Tom's angry tone turned to a scream.) Where is she. Tell me where is she is!.

CHARLES: (Losing patience.) Don't you talk to me like that. You mistreat my sister for half of her life. You force her out. And then you demand I give her away. No chance.

TOM: (Half a country away, Tom Boyle was red faced and furious.) You will tell me where she is or I'll come over. . .

The line dropped out. Boyle's furious mind concentrated on two objects: how to find Ada, and fixing Charles.

Three weeks later.

Rhonda prodded Charles. There was someone at the front door. It was two o'clock in the morning. Charles forced himself out of bed and walked over to a chair and groped for a pair of shorts. The doorbell rang again.

Charles opened the door to see a man in shirt sleeves, stomach bulging over knee length shorts.

"You call a taxi?"

Charles was still asleep. He shook his head and closed the door.

The next night the episode was repeated. Same time. Same type of shorts. However the visitor was not a taxi driver:

"You call a tow-truck, mate?"

Charles returned to bed, and sat up thinking. He nudged Rhonda, who had returned to the land of dreams.

"Rhonda", he nudged Rhonda. "I think someone's having a lend of us."

With a settling, "Let's talk about it in the morning, love", Rhonda rolled over and all was silent once more.

The doorbell rang.

"Oh, give me a break!" Charles threw himself out of bed and darted to the door, calling as he went. "Who is it this time, the pizza delivery man?" He flung the door open, and a small balding man in glasses and a cheap business suit stood unassumingly in the light.

"Excuse me, is this Charlie's Massage Parlour?"

The man was pulled in the door by the collar and forced to sit down on the lounge.

For the next half hour the man was given treatment very unlike that of his expectations. Where did he get the address? Who told him this was a massage parlour?

Eventually the frightened little man described posters which had been put up all around the neighbouring suburbs. Cheap rates they promised. Good service.

The balding man was then out on the street. He'd never been to a massage parlour before. Probably never risk going to one again. He went home to his beefy, bullying wife. At least it was safe there.

Charles was already on the phone to the police.

The tow-truck driver, the taxi and the massage parlour posters incidents were all explained to the constable on the line. For some reason the jovial young officer thought it necessary to have Charles repeat the story to two or three other constables. At the end of the call, the officer suggested Charles drop around in the morning to put in an official complaint. Maybe if they could find one of the posters, they might be able to trace the harasser.

The next day Charles sat down with a sergeant for fifteen minutes. It wasn't until the officer asked if there was anyone who might have had a grudge against him, that Charles thought of Tom Boyle. Boyle had been pretty angry. But again he was in Adelaide. Charles told the officer about Ada's break-up, and the phone threat. Tom Boyle didn't know where Ada was, but he knew where Charles lived.

The sergeant promised to check with the Adelaide police, but said there was not a great deal that could be done. Unless Tom confessed, or left some tell-tale sign on the posters, Tom was untouchable.

Charles went home.

As he pulled into his street he brightened. The council must finally be doing some work on the road – he could see earth blocking the footpath down the street near their home.

It wasn't until he was about to go into his driveway that Charles realised the earth was not only on the footpath, but in his front yard as well, blocking the front door and preventing the car from getting to the carport.

The police were quickly on the scene. Four constables came out of the unmarked vehicle. Two of them burst into laughter and got back into the car.

Investigations would proceed immediately.

After this Charles found great difficulty sleeping. Every sound outside the house would propel him out of the bed. Their phone number had been changed at the suggestion of the police. This stopped the late night calls. Now taxis and tow trucks would pull up out the front and beep their horns. The police spoke to the drivers, but all they were able to say was that they had received late emergency calls from callers who provided, as it turned out, false names.

About a month after the soil was dumped Rhonda nudged her husband who jumped out of bed. "What? What is it?"

"I heard someone. . . " Her words were cut off by a crash of glass and a flash of fire in their bedroom.

"Get out Rhonda, quick! I'll try and douse it."

Tom Boyle was arrested a few days later. He denied throwing anything through the window of his brother-in-law's house. Besides, he claimed, he was in a different State at the time.

Boyle was committed for trial. He stood in the dock enclosed in the sandstone walls of the Supreme Court and listened as Charles gave him a character reference.

Charles told the jury that Tom was a violent man, had fits of temper, was abusive and impolite.

Charles told how he had lived with Tom and Ada for some months in South Australia, and how he wished he hadn't.

Tom Boyle gave the jury a different version. He stood uncomfortably in his blue suit and tie, and told the jury he had been framed.

Indeed, he said, it was not he who committed the outrages. Poor Tom was a victim. He had been harassed himself. Charles had dumped soil on *his* driveway, not the other way around. Charles had belted him up. Tom had been a model husband. For twenty years he'd doted, loved and indulged his wife Ada. And then Charles comes and takes her away. Tears her away from the man she adores. No, Tom wasn't the aggressor, he was the victim. Something ought to be done about interfering in-laws.

Tom's plea to the jury might have been effective, if Ada had not given evidence.

Ada told the court Tom and Black Beard could have been related. She said the twenty years of marriage had been something akin to a long sentence in a maximum security prison. Tom was a vile, abusive, dirty creep with poor personal hygiene. The woman burst into tears as she described how she had to beg her brother Charles to save her from Tom Boyle. The court was asked to keep Tom away from her for a long time.

The Supreme Court jury took just fifteen minutes to agree to the request.

THE NON-DRINK DRIVER

Some police cases appear so secure that foolish prosecutors will claim they are "in the bag". The evidence against the charged person seems to be so strong that nothing could prevent a guilty finding. Fred Kowalski was one of the few to prove that even the best prepared cases can be beaten. . .

"Great bunch o' fellas!" thought Fred.

As usual, the pub crowd had enlivened Ted Kowalski's Friday night. It was now late. He had spent longer at the Royal than he'd intended, but the commonsense characters, the political chatter and the eccentrics were hard to leave.

There was Jack, a Czech refugee. Mad as a hatter. Always so emotional, so fervent and outspoken on political matters. He was a mess of laughter and anger. Nobody took Jack too seriously, but everybody liked him.

Or Spiros, the bible-bashing Greek who claimed he only ever visited the pub in an effort to distract his workmates from the drink. Great bunch o' fellas.

Ted knew he had to be careful. It had been raining and the road easily turned to dirt. In these conditions, the ute became hard to handle. . .

Ted woke in hospital. His chest and his back were hurting. A male nurse tending a bed on the other side of the room looked over at Ted and called for the matron.

Soon the matron was by his bed, asking him how he felt. Ted told her he hurt and asked what had happened.

The matron told him he had hit a pole on the dirt road. There were no other casualties, but Ted had damaged his back and breast bone. She also said she was surprised Ted couldn't remember, because he had extricated himself from the wreck, walked home, and then been brought to the hospital by his wife Steffie. It was only while being treated by the doctor that he had fainted. Up until then he seemed completely lucid.

Never mind, she said. The memory about the accident would probably come back later. The injuries weren't too bad – she'd seen a lot worse. In all he was pretty lucky. . . the ute was a write-off. He would probably only be off work for a little while.

Oh yes, the matron said the police wanted to interview him about the accident. Would he mind if she called them straight away? Best to get it out of the way. They'd be over soon.

Ted lay back in the sheets. He couldn't remember anything about an accident. He could recall the night at the pub; the fellas, the songs, the political shouting matches, but not the crash. He certainly couldn't remember anything about walking home.

He told the same thing to the two police officers who stood by the bed.

The woman officer asked Ted how much he had been drinking on the night of the accident. Ted said he could remember having a few light beers. He wasn't a big drinker, he said. He had some whiskey at home for use on special occasions, but he didn't like drink as a rule.

The male officer then informed Ted that a sample of his blood, taken when he was admitted, had shown he was four times over the legal driving limit. Since he had walked for an hour from the car, and rested at home for a short while, he would have been a lot higher at the time of the crash.

Ted insisted the machinery was wrong.

The officers insisted the machinery was right.

It was left to a court to decide.

The prosecutor's outline of the charge case seemed to present a tight case. Ted had been in an accident. Two hours had passed, and he still registered a high blood alcohol reading.

Magistrate Shirley Simmons asked Ted if he wanted to present any evidence on his own behalf. He answered yes, and asked if some of the drinkers from the Royal could take the stand.

Russell was first. He swore that Ted was very sober when he left to drive home that night. He told Magistrate Simmons that Ted had been in every shout, but had only ordered a drink for himself every third round. . . and it was always a light beer. "He'd 'af ta drink a gallon of that muck to get boozed!"

Jack the refugee followed Russell onto the stand. Jack told the magistrate how upset he was that his good friend Ted was before the court. He said that if Ted was to be thrown in prison, he would go too. Ted would not be alone in this crisis.

Jack had to be escorted from the stand.

Willie followed. Willie was the "straight" member of the pub group. An accountant by day, Willie took charge of the payments for the shouts. Everybody in the group could give Willie ten or twenty dollars at the beginning of the night and he would calculate – without error – how much each was to receive back after the rounds had finished. Willie had an enormous memory, and often entertained the pub by reciting football teams from the

1940s, as well as Melbourne Cup winners, and members of State and Federal cabinets. . . and their birthdates.

Willie told the magistrate that Ted had three light beers at the pub that night.

The prosecutor tried to shift Willie's evidence. It was not negotiable. The prosecutor did not know Willie.

The magistrate said she was impressed by the evidence of the three men, but she said this still didn't explain the high presence of alcohol in Ted's system. The prosecutor gave a barely audible “hear hear”.

But Ted then asked if his wife Steffie could give testimony.

The magistrate was reluctant. She asked Ted the relevance of Steffie's evidence. Ted said she could help prove he was sober at the time of the accident.

The evidence was allowed, over the objection of the prosecutor. Steffie told Magistrate Simmons that on the night of the accident she was doing some ironing. It was Friday night and Ted was usually late on Fridays because it was pub night.

Steffie said there was a knock at the door, and she answered it to find Ted standing there, with blood all over his shirt and a gash on his forehead.

Ted was brought inside the house, and made to lie on the lounge. The head wound had stopped bleeding, and Steffie started mopping up the dried blood.

That was when she gave him the scotches.

The prosecutor and the magistrate, both of whom had been settling back into the chairs, were sparked into instant attention. Magistrate Simmons asked Steffie how many scotches she gave to her husband.

Three. Oh yes, and a brandy. She ran out of scotch after the third one had been poured.

After the brandy had been administered, the injured Ted had relaxed, claiming the wounds to be superficial. But Steffie said she forced him to go to hospital to have the injuries checked out. It was only when Ted stood that she noticed the black bruising on his chest. He became very drowsy in the car, but that was probably due to all the alcohol. He couldn't handle alcohol, Ted.

The magistrate said that in the end it came down to whether she believed the evidence of Mrs Kowalski and the witnesses from the pub.

After careful deliberation Ms Simmons said she felt all these witnesses were telling the truth. They had said nothing which contradicted the police evidence. They just offered a rational alternative explanation for the high blood reading. The charge was dismissed, and Ted was told he was free to go. He was instantly swamped by Russell, Jack and Willie. Jack was in tears – authority had been beaten.

Russell and Willie lifted Ted onto their shoulders and carried the embarrassed man through the court foyer out onto the street.

They did their real celebrating at the local.

BUT THEY'RE MY BABIES!

In court you see all kinds of people. And all kinds of people do all kinds of things, and make all kinds of choices. The notorious case of Mrs Hardacre illustrates the point.

Jack Hardacre had lived on an island off the North Coast of New South Wales for some years. He'd moved there after his wife died. The loss had been so distressing that Jack had decided to throw in the city life and move somewhere quieter. A business associate suggested the island. There seemed to be few drawbacks to the change, so for the first time in his life he acted impulsively and moved offshore.

Life on the island was better than he had anticipated. Jack became ensconced in the island's easy pace.

But he still missed his wife.

He returned to the mainland for his son's wedding. At the reception he was a celebrity. People kept asking him about the island. How did he do without toilets? He must be strong willed to manage without electricity.

Jack explained that the island was not all jungle. That it had modern areas and that, yes, there was even electricity.

"Dad, I want you to meet Lorna. She's Donna's sister's mother-in-law."

The pink-faced woman smiled at Jack. "How do you do, Mr Hardacre? They tell me that you live on an island. How exciting. I've always wanted to do something so. . . so. . . native. But tell me, how do you get on without electricity?"

The woman was pushy, but she attracted Jack. That impulsive feeling – the feeling that had changed his life – again guided his actions. Jack and Lorna married a few weeks later.

It was on the dock that Lorna introduced Jack to her two "children", Peachy and Clarence. Jack didn't know much about cats. He guessed they were Siamese, or something.

Some months later, their neighbour on the island came storming up to the house.

"You had no right to bring those bloody cats of yours here. They're chasing the bushrats and possums."

Lorna could see this woman was plainly without manners. And what was worse, had no style.

"Oh, don't be stupid. The darlings won't eat anything other than 'Sardines in Aspic'."

A day later a pimply faced messenger delivered a message. Jack and Lorna were to go to the local government office in the civic centre in two days' time.

Lorna's maternal hackles rose: "I bet that alternative person from next door complained about Clarence and Peachy. Summon me, will they? They aren't doing anything to my babies. We didn't put up with any rubbish like this in Woollahra".

Jack liked the neighbours. "Darling, I'm sure Mary wouldn't cause any trouble. What if I just go talk to her and find out."

"Talk to her nothing, Jack Hardacre. I'll fix that back-to-nature nut!"

Lorna's confidence was boosted at the sight of the small, simple office building. Jack touched Lorna's arm: "Darling, let's just hear what they have to say. . ." Lorna jerked her arm away: "They'll hear what I have to say first!".

The three members of the board listened as Lorna told them about her rights as a citizen, and about how the cats were not causing any problems.

"What cats?", the slim, well-tanned and weathered-looking man in the centre interrupted. "We wanted to talk to you about your status on the island. Just routine. But tell us. What cats?"

Jack poked his wife in the back. She hit his hand with a backward swing: "My babies. The two Siamese I brought with me from the mainland".

"But where did you get permission to bring cats onto the island?"

"Why the man at the dock said it was okay."

"Mrs Hardacre, are you aware this island has a no cats policy?"

"A no what?"

"A no cats policy. No cats can be brought onto this island. It is a law. No exceptions."

Lorna reddened: "Well you will have to make an exception. My babies have lived here for months. They love it here. I live here. We are newly-weds."

She looked towards Jack. The others looked at Jack too. The look was one of collective sympathy. Jack gathered that their sympathy had nothing to do with the cats.

"I'm sorry." The slim man was adamant. "No choice. They must be removed immediately."

Lorna shrugged off Jack's arm:

"Look at the three of you sitting there like a bunch of cockatoos! Trying to tell me to give up my babies! I'll see you in court!"

That night Lorna spoke by phone to a Queen's Counsel she had met at a cocktail party the year before.

After inquiring about how she got on without electricity, the barrister agreed to look into the matter.

The Supreme Court, Sydney.

Justice Maree Nordup was told about the fauna laws. She was told that the cats had relaxed into the island's lifestyle. She smirked, imagining the felines doing the rumba to the click of maracas. She had little choice. The law was the law.

She gave her decision. Lorna didn't take it well: "What are you saying? I have to give up my babies? Is that what you're saying?".

The judge wanted to placate Lorna. She was about to attempt some response when she saw her associate Sidney had turned and was looking up at her with that expectant smile. "Let's see you sort this one out Maree", he would be thinking.

The judge took her glasses off, and then put them back on. "Mrs Hardacre. . ." She took her glasses off. "Mrs Hardacre, I. . ." The urge to replace the glasses was overwhelming. She decided it best to say nothing else.

The court was adjourned. It was now up to Lorna and Jack.

Still, she wondered whether the woman really did choose the cats over her husband.

A few months later Sidney came into chambers.

SIDNEY: Judge, do you remember that case about the island and the cats?

JUSTICE NORDUP: (Dropping her pen.) Yes, yes. What do you know?

SIDNEY: I've been told she took a flat in Sydney.

The judge thought about whether she should ask. . . Oh, what the hell!

JUSTICE NORDUP: She chose the cats?
SIDNEY: You got it boss!

She shook her head and picked up her pen. Cases were waiting.

THE LATIN LOVER

People impersonate others for many reasons – some want money which isn't their own, others want access to restricted places. A third kind of impersonator is after prestige with all the resultant perks – and Mr Waan was one of the these.

It was Friday night at Julio's Castanet Club. The music was so loud you couldn't hear anyone who was more than six inches away; the room was full of smoke and was so crowded that it was impossible to appreciate the designer dresses in abundance that night. Cathy and Samantha were sitting at the bar. They had arrived at about eight, and for the past hour they had already prised themselves away from the ambitious advances of at least six men. Usually the approaches were instantaneous. No gazing from across the room. . . no offers of a drink through the bar operator. Men just came into the club, saw the women and tried their luck. Many of them did not even try to conceal the wedding ring. So it was unusual that the small man at the other end of the bar sat there eyeing them off quite boldly. He seemed to have endless patience (compared with the other men in the place anyway).

Soon the two women started discussing this man. Would he make a pass? Was he one of those who was satisfied just by getting your interest? Or was he looking at that bloke sitting behind them? The girls didn't know why they cared. The man was strange-looking – not ugly – but again, no oil painting as they say. He was too old for them anyway. Samantha, who had a direct line of vision with the gazer, tapped Cathy on the sleeve and looked down. This older, non-oil-painting was making his move.

Up close, he was older, and wouldn't even have been a watercolour. He asked them if they were enjoying the evening. Samantha and Cathy were offhand. They said they were indeed having a lovely night. While they had enjoyed this man's obvious interest from afar, the pleasure had diminished now that he was within conversation range. He was also a lot shorter than he looked from a distance (he was shorter than both women – and they were sitting on stools).

He asked Samantha if she cared to dance. Samantha said she would have loved to, except that her husband was just on the other side of the room with his mates from the Tae Kwon Do school.

This little fib worked. The hopeful Casanova turned his attention to Cathy. Would *she* care to dance. Cathy was more honest. She simply thanked the small man for his interest and declined the offer at this time.

His countenance changed. Confident composure was replaced by indignation. He told them that he was a police officer – Senior Constable Inspector Detective Waan from the Wollongong Police Force. With this piece of information the man pulled an identification card with "NSW Police Department" stamped across the bottom. The current commissioner's signature and the state government seal graced the corner of the card.

He could see both women were unimpressed with this piece of information (women these days have no respect for authority). With this Senior ConstableInspector Detective Waan undid his coat button and pulled open the left side to reveal a leather holster and the butt of a gun protruding. He asked them whether they were impressed. They said they had to go to the powder room.

While Senior Constable Inspector Detective Waan waited at the bar congratulating himself on the mastery of his technique, the women went into the powder room marked "manager's office".

Ten minutes later two uniformed police officers entered the office and asked Samantha and Cathy to point out the man with the gun. They poked their heads through the manager's door and pointed to Senior Constable Inspector Detective Waan, who was still waiting at the bar, and running a comb through his hair.

He turned around and saw Cathy pointing him out to the uniformed police. He dropped the comb and dashed to the male powder room.

Carefully, the officers followed the well-combed man into the toilet. There was no sign of him, but a cubicle was shut. One of the officers got down on his knees and put his cheek to the floor. That was the bloke – although only the bottom of the pants were visible, the magenta-coloured suit was unmistakable. The shoes were quaking.

The officer stood and asked the man if he had a gun. The nervous voice replied in the affirmative – but said it was only a toy he bought for his son. The officers asked the man to slide the gun under the door. This was done. He was then asked to come out, and were answered with a petulant: "No. And you can't make me!".

One of the officers put his arm over the cubicle door and unlocked it. Senior Constable Inspector Detective Waan was sitting, quaking, on the toilet seat. He handed over the empty holster and accompanied the officers to the nearby police centre.

As he walked in, a superintendent called out a greeting to the budding Casanova. The officers became worried. Was there a special department in Wollongong? If so, then oops!

The man was thoroughly searched, and the identification card was found. A desk sergeant examined the card closely. It certainly was NSW police issue, but liquid paper had been applied over the top of one section. One top of this correction fluid the station: "Senior Constable Inspector Detective Waan" had been scrawled in using a biro.

After the card was photographed, the officers scraped away the liquid paper and found the so-called detective's true rank: "Cleaning Contractor"

It turned out that the man had altered the card some time before, but had never had the courage to actually use it. On the night in question seven whiskeys had given him the courage to try out his "sure-fire" girl catcher.

Waan was charged with impersonating a police officer. He later pleaded guilty and was fined.

PS Waan was the man's real surname. The first name was one of those incredible coincidences that only ever come up in court: Don.

Don Waan.

BIG JIM HOLDS COURT

As a reporter, I'm looking for a good yarn – something everyone will want to hear about and will talk about at dinner tables. Courts can reveal some of the most tragic stories imaginable. But they can also be so entertaining, you would wish it were on film.

A circle of television cameras and reporters in various styles of dress were forming a huddle on the footpath, all desperate for a quick quip, quotable quote, good angle shot and a story for the lunchtime bulletin. They call it a "feeding frenzy".

The centre of the attention was one of those people everybody knows: prominent investigator Jim Lennon, summonsed to the seaside courthouse on a charge of possessing an unlicensed pistol.

Jim, who had managed to avoid serious criminal charges through all of his seventy-two years, was able to disparage the charge and its sponsors. Big Jim was one of the master actors.

"A bloody joke. That's what it is. A bloody joke!" Jim looked around during a dramatic pause. The journalists smiled at Jim's indignation.

Jim was at that stage of life where he no longer took himself seriously. These public comments were not intended to put pressure on the police. He was just having a bit of fun.

"When I get into this courthouse, I'm going to tell the magistrate just as much too!" Another scan at the throng. More smiles.

The Channel Nine cub reporter had, with all the seriousness of a budding Willesee, kept his frown, listening intently to every word. Verbal gold. Every word gold. History.

"Mr Lennon, are you saying you are being victimised?"

The remaining throng mentally groan – all thinking that there is always at least one turkey who takes these things seriously.

Big Jim looks set to answer.

Collective smiles disappear, replaced by frowns. The microphones mover closer. The Channel Seven cameraman pushes a radio reporter's microphone down a little, out of the picture.

"Well", Jim takes his time, and adds to the tension. "You just wait to hear what I have to say to the magistrate! But this case is bloody ridiculous!"

The questions end without eliciting the quote we need so we can file a quick story and go for a cappuccino. The group disbands. Jim goes over to talk to two men who have been standing on the fringe of the huddle.

A colleague asks me if I think they are Jim's bodyguards. Both men look pleasant enough. They wear worn jeans and tee-shirts. They are underweight and generally unhealthy. In fact although Jim passed their ages about thirty years ago, he is the one who looks more like the bodyguard.

We go in to get a ringside seat.

As usual, the case we are after is about tenth down the list.

The magistrate hardly takes his eyes away from the pieces of paper put down in front of him. He knows he has about sixty cases to dispose of this morning. No cappuccinos for him.

MAGISTRATE: Okay Sergeant, who's next?

The slim well-muscled sergeant with a crew cut, dressed in a light blue single-breasted special, stands.

SERGEANT: Charge case number seven, Your Worship. James McCartney.

The junior reporter from the local daily nudges me, obviously trying to impress with his prowess.

"That's him!"

"No, mate", I tell him, "We're waiting for Lennon. Wrong Beatle".

The news reporters were lined up in the front row of the public gallery. Notebooks on laps, pens held two inches above the paper. The male reporters are leaning forward, legs apart, knees quivering. Anticipation.

One reporter starts taking notes as the sergeant reads out the details of the current case. . . that of a 35-year-old accountant caught drink-driving.

One by one, like cattle who have sniffed a far off waterhole in a drought, the other reporters lift their heads and see the first journalist writing. After a moment they too are taking notes. Later that day all the news stations will tell the world about an unfortunate accountant who had one too many. Even being on the same court list as Jim Lennon can ruin a life.

COURT OFFICER: James George MacCafferty Lennon!

As soon as the officer called out the name, Jim Lennon strode from outside the court, through the gallery to the stand. He didn't need directions.

BIG JIM: Your Worship, I just want to say this is all garbage. It had nothing to do with me. It's not even my gun. It's a case of police being malicious.

The magistrate nodded throughout the tirade, obviously waiting for an opportunity to butt in.

MAGISTRATE: All right. Sergeant, what are the facts in the police case?

The slim man in the single-breasted suit stood. One hand in pocket, he stood towering over two pages spread on the table in front of him.

SERGEANT: Simply these Your Worship: on 22 March of this year, following an anonymous call to local police, a search warrant was sought by detectives for the premises of James Lennon.

At eight o'clock that night a team of seventeen detectives executed the said warrant. Inside a drawer in a wardrobe in the second bedroom of the house, a point-four-five revolver was found.

Mr Lennon was formally arrested and conveyed to the local police station where he formally refused to participate in a police record of interview.

His solicitor was contacted and Mr Lennon was released on bail after being charged with possessing an unlicensed gun.

Your Worship, a check of police records has shown that Mr Lennon is not currently in possession of a gun licence for this particular weapon.

The sergeant resumed his seat. All eyes in the court returned to Jim Lennon, who was still standing at the opposite side of the room.

The magistrate made a few notes and then turned to Big Jim.

> *MAGISTRATE:* What do you have to say about the allegations Mr Lennon?

Lines were drawn across the pages of the reporters' notebooks. They had just received the police version. Jim's side of things was always different and invariably more interesting.

Big Jim stuck out his chest.

> *BIG JIM:* A bloody joke this is, if I may say so. First of all the bloody gun's more than sixty years old. Check on it yourself. Besides, it doesn't even work! It's rusty, for goodness sake! A bit fell off it the other day.

Alternating the direction of his comments between the magistrate and the media, Big Jim deepened his voice and clenched his fists.

> *BIG JIM:* I didn't think you needed a gun licence for something that doesn't even work! If I was going to do someone in, I wouldn't use a rusty gun. It'd blow up in me face!

The magistrate was writing all this down. During the last comment he lifted his eyebrows, but kept writing.

> *BIG JIM:* Another thing Your Worship, *(shifting again to a deep, emphasized voice)* I don't even own the bloody gun. It belongs to my mate Spike.

With this Jim turned to the back of the court and lifted one of his well-muscled, but ageing arms.

> *BIG JIM:* Hey Spike, stand up and tell 'im it's yours!

One of the jeaned supporters stood. . . right on cue. The magistrate told him to sit down and asked Big Jim to dispense with the histrionics.

> *BIG JIM: (Feigning shock.)* But it's not even mine! How can I be charged when the thing doesn't work, and it doesn't even belong to me?
>
> *MAGISTRATE:* Thank you Mr Lennon. I stand this matter over to 15 June for a plea or mention.

Of course we all turned up to Big Jim's next court appearance. The magistrate at the next hearing obviously sympathised with Big Jim's indignation and the charge was thrown out.

After all the drama, the feeding frenzy and the tension, Big Jim got off leaving us with no story. Nothing. Zot.

The police, who thought they had finally caught the big man, were disappointed too, but philosophical. One of them said he would obviously have wanted to have had Jim convicted, but added:

"You could pay twenty dollars and go to the theatre, but still not be as entertained as when you're watching Big Jim demolish a carefully constructed police case with his dramatics and simple small-town philosophy."

I laughed, and turned to see Big Jim walking towards us. As he passed he nodded to me: "Loverly day, mate".

I looked skywards. It was overcast and cold. "Yes, it is nice."

You just *didn't* disagree with Big Jim.

On any subject.

ROBBER REPENTS

Apart from punishing offenders and protecting the community, our sentencing system is also designed to deter people from committing offences. In one case, a young man was sorry for his misdeeds – but arguably, for the wrong reason.

Gus was an intelligent and articulate young man who unfortunately had devoted his teenage years to fighting battles against the agents of the law. As a result, his record was long and interesting. Experience had given the young man a range of tactics which he used in usually unsuccessful attempts, to "beat the rap".

This time, Gus was up for appeal against a thirteen-year sentence for armed robbery. Disillusioned with a legal profession unable to free the guilty, Gus decided to speak for himself in the appeal.

The three Court of Criminal Appeal judges filed into the Banco Court. The Crown prosecutor and his solicitor sat on one side of the bar table. Barristers, waiting for their own cases sat behind the prosecutor, and checked their papers.

Gus was brought into the dock, and the chief judge asked the Crown to outline the history of the case.

> *PROSECUTOR:* The prisoner was arrested in Sydney last month. Inquiries confirmed that at the time of the arrest he was on the run from authorities in two States. He had just broken out of an interstate prison where he had been serving a twenty-five-year sentence for robbery. . .

The judges were then told that this appeal was over a series of armed robberies Gus had carried out on banks and a TAB agency.

The Chief Justice leaned forward and asked Gus what would be the basis of the appeal.

> *GUS:* Yer Hons, I don't have any qualms with the convictions. I mean, fair enough. I did the jobs. I got caught. Que sera and laissez faire. But *thirteen years*? That's a bit stiff!

Gus addressed the judges with the perverse logic of someone who has dallied with the wigged and gowned before.

> *GUS:* Yer Hons, I didn't realise that I could be jailed for so long for simple armed robberies. I think it's a little unfair to jail me for this long when I thought I'd only get a few years. After all, isn't our justice system all about fairness?

The judges were obviously entertained by the enterprising young man before them. Certainly the freshness of the arguments maintained their attention.

> *GUS:* So, Yer Hons, I want you to see that it's unfair for me to be jailed for this long, when I only expected a few years. If the courts want to deter us from crime, then the courts should be consistent.

One of the judges ventured into the argument.

> *JUDGE TWO:* So you're saying that if you had known the sentence was going to be so long, you would not have robbed the banks or the TAB.

The prisoner brightened:

> *GUS:* That's right Yer Hon, I would have gone down the street and broken into a few houses instead. . .

Gus is still serving his thirteen years.

WHO LIT THE FIRE?

Some people fight court cases under the assumption that the judges, jury and opposing counsel have a collective IQ in the single-digit range. When these people lose the case they are (as you would expect) usually shocked at the result. This is such a case.

"I was at home relaxing with my wife, when the police told me my business had burned down. It was a great shock, let me tell you."

John Babbas had just started his evidence in the dock of the Supreme Court. He was suing Takya Cash Insurers. They were refusing to pay his claim for two million dollars. His claim was over his family hardware store which had been burnt out by a fire.

The insurers believed there had been some monkey business. This fire, they claimed, was no accident. John Babbas strongly disagreed:

> *BABBAS:* I thought, "Oh no, my business! The business I have built over ten years. All come to nothing". That business, I tell you, was my life. Even now, I cannot find the words to describe my pain.

John was being questioned by Rex Butler QC, the doyen of the barristers. He was representing the insurance company. He was not only feared by his adversaries, but feted by all the insurance houses. He charged a fortune, but Rex, with his penetrating stare and focussed mind, was a winner and that was all that counted. This was the man who, in the great Bank trial of 1967, brought tears to the courtroom. Not tears from the witness, or the public gallery, but from his opposing barrister. Yes, Rex was a powerhouse.

Rex had been waiting to examine John Babbas for six months. He wanted this man in the stand. Rex wanted to consume, decimate, devastate.

The time had come.

> *BUTLER:* Mr Babbas, what time did you leave work on the evening of the fire?

The witness needed no time to ponder his answer.

> *BABBAS:* At 5.45 pm.

The barristerial barracuda stared at the witness.

> *BUTLER:* And how did you get home that evening?
>
> *BABBAS:* I drove. How else would I. . .
>
> *BUTLER:* Then why was your vehicle parked outside the back gate to the building at 6.20 pm – the estimated time the fire was lit?

The witness keeled over, clutching his stomach

> *BABBAS:* Your Honour, I am feeling ill. It suddenly hit me. I. . .

The judge asked if a glass of water would ease the discomfort. John Babbas carefully explained how the pain usually lasted for at least an hour. He was sorry but he would have to leave the court. There was no choice. John Babbas limped from the witness stand.

Rather than interrupt the evidence, Rex asked that his other witnesses be called.

The first in the box were the insurance investigators. They told the court that false evidence trails had been carefully laid within the burning building. Padlocks had been smashed, litter scattered. All designed to make the investigators think the fire was an act of wanton arson by an individual.

The police were called. They gave evidence that despite the broken padlocks, the building was entered through the back door, with a key being used.

The company which installed the alarm system was called to give evidence. The installer told the court that the alarm system was turned off prior to the break in. There had been no fiddling with the alarm box. It had been turned off using a remote control. The only control which could have done this was the owner's one.

Rex Butler tightened the noose around the Babbas family by calling financial investigators to the stand. They told the court that John Babbas and his sister were in a parlous financial state. Liabilities grossly exceeded assets. In other words, they were strapped for cash.

Next, with great anticipation, Rex had his chance to examine Joanne Babbas, John's sister.

The slight, dark-eyed woman walked to the box.

Rex started by asking her if her stomach was all right. In reply he was told she had a bad back and a hernia.

The woman was asked whether, on the fateful night, she had switched on the building's security system.

> *JOANNE BABBAS:* Yes. I always switch on the security system before John and I leave.
>
> *BUTLER:* How do you do this?
>
> *JOANNE BABBAS:* I press the buttons on my remote control.
>
> *BUTLER:* I see. Who, besides yourself, has a remote control?
>
> *JOANNE BABBAS:* Only John.
>
> *BUTLER:* Thank you Miss Babbas. Oh, by the way, who has keys to the building?
>
> *JOANNE BABBAS:* Only John and myself.

Rex continued:

BUTLER: Miss Babbas. You were in the court when we heard evidence from independent security experts that the break-in must have been effected using a key, and the alarm system must have been turned off with the remote control?

JOANNE BABBAS: Er, yes.

BUTLER: So how did the arsonists get a remote alarm control and a key?

JOANNE BABBAS: They must have made copies!

BUTLER: Miss Babbas, how do you copy a remote control?

JOANNE BABBAS: Ooh. My migraine! It just hit me. I'm in agony!

The insurance company representatives didn't turn up to hear the rest of the carefully constructed demolition job after lunch that day. Too much champagne had made them a little queasy.

PSST! WANNA BUY A SNAKE?

This story has no moral. No legal significance. No anything. But it could only happen in Australia.

The sergeant called the two officers to a quiet desk at the back of the station.

> *SERGEANT:* Look fellers, we've got a delicate situation down at the Stag's Head. Seems a bloke has this bloody big snake in a bag, and he's trying to sell it. It's just my luck that I happen to be on duty when the call comes through. And it's just *your* luck that I'm sending you out to pick up the man *and* his snake.

The constables thought the sarge was joking and giggled along. The sarge wasn't joking.

> *CONSTABLE SMITH:* Aw, c'mon sarge. They didn't tell us nothin' at the academy about handling snakes. . .
> *CONSTABLE JONES:* I bags arrestin' the bloke. Smithy can get the adder.
> *SERGEANT:* I don't care who gets the snake. But whoever it is, be careful. We're short staffed as it is. . .

Meanwhile, at the Stag's Head. . .

The man had been showing the snake around for about twenty minutes. If he wasn't an illegal trader, he at least looked the part. He wore a white trench-style coat. His hair was brushed back off his forehead and wore designer sunglasses. He was a calm character. This was just as well, because any panic would have cleared the pub in ten seconds, beer or no beer.

The carpet adder matched it's calm owner, staying quietly coiled in the hessian bag. The man wanted serious money for the reptile, but so far he had only been offered a six pack. Snakes were not big business in inner city pubs. This was the third hotel visited by the snake-bearer. The man had expected a quick sale – ready cash. No questions asked. Great! Two hours he'd carted the thing around. It wasn't just the money... what do you do with a snake that no-one wants?

Ted Hawke leaned on the bar. He was tired. He'd had a stressful day at the agency. Ever since lunchtime he had been wanting to knock off and have a couple of beers at the Stag's Head. Ted took his sips as he watched the television above the bar. He didn't hear somebody call out that the cops were in the pub. Ted took another drink. . .

The man on the next stool asked Ted if he would mind his bag for a minute while he went to the toilet. Sure, Ted said, just leave it on the floor. No, the man replied, would Ted mind holding it on his lap? He didn't want it to get dirty. Alright. Ted didn't see the man go straight out onto the street. He also never saw if the man came back. Thirty seconds after being given custody of the bag, Ted was arrested.

Back at the station:

TED: This is ridiculous. It wasn't my bag I'm telling you!

SERGEANT: Right. I understand. You were minding the snake for a friend. . .

TED: No. I keep telling you. I never saw the bloke before in my life.

SERGEANT: I see. You just like minding snakes which belong to perfect strangers, eh?

TED: I didn't know what was in the bag.

SERGEANT: It was a carpet python. . . three metres long, and weighed the same as a small child. What did you think the bag contained. Bricks?

The sergeant obviously didn't believe Ted. Magistrate Sally McPherson didn't know what to think. But in the end she said the pass-the-bag story was so unbelievable, it had to be true. Ted was not convicted on a charge of taking the snake from the wild, but was fined seventy-five dollars for possessing the snake in public. It was more likely a punishment for being naive in a pub of hard knocks.

PS Despite their apprehension, constables Smith and Jones developed quite some affection for the carpet python. A policewoman at the station who was from the bush pronounced the snake safe for handling. It was named Monty and stayed as station mascot for two days while wildlife authorities arranged a pick-up. One of the officers even asked the sergeant if he could keep him, but Monty was eventually released into a nearby national park. Monty probably never had a clue about all the trouble he had caused.

KNUCKLEDUSTERS

This is an example of how, sometimes, things can just get out of hand.

It all began with a simple accident in Sydney's inner city. A car and a van met violently at an intersection early in the morning. No-one was seriously injured, but several passengers were taken to hospital for X-rays and observation.

Harold was one of the injured. A few hours after the accident he was lying in a ward bed counting his good fortune. For a twisted ankle, he was getting free board and a little sympathy from the nurses.

Then suddenly Harold had a sinking feeling. He reached for the drawer where his wallet and shopping bag had been stowed by the hospital staff. A search didn't reveal what he was looking for, so he pulled the drawer out and furiously tore through its contents. He fell back on his pillow.

He had left his knuckledusters in the van.

The whole scenario ran through his mind. The police would be sure to go through the vehicle, trying to work out the cause of the accident. The illegal knuckledusters would be discovered. An investigation would ensue, his ownership uncovered, and a criminal charge and possible jail would result. Especially with his record.

Harold decided to try to get to the knuckledusters before the cops.

Over the protestations of the nurses, he hobbled to the red phone in the corridor, fumbled the change into the machine and rang an acquaintance of his – a well-known businessman, a man with apparent connections in the right places.

The plight was carefully explained. The businessman, feeling some sympathy for his distant acquaintance, and always happy to be owed a favour, then rang a detective at the police station closest to the scene of the accident.

It was a crazy day. Detective Bill Luckett was up to his eyeballs in drug and robbery investigations. Real crime. He barked out orders to the junior officers while, out of the phone earpiece, the businessman rattled forth about the knuckledusters. Bill's only responses was an occasional grunt.

The businessman then put on the pinch for assistance.

Bill had more important things to do besides listening to some unsavoury bloke trying to earn a favour from a mate. But he was a good contact, so Bill said he'd look into the matter, and promptly did nothing.

Unfortunately for the sergeant, the phone to this particular police station had been tapped by the powers-that-be, who were investigating a completely different matter. The fact that this conversation was recorded was pure chance (or ill-luck).

Because of the detective's words of promise, a prosecution was started against him.

The dominoes started falling in earnest. The detective was committed for trial in the district court on a charge of conspiracy to pervert the course of justice.

To be convicted on a conspiracy charge, a person does not have to actually carry out the crime – just agree with another person to do it. Technically, that was what Detective Bill Luckett did – he agreed to pervert the course of justice, on the phone, on tape, on record, on a boat down the river.

Detective Bill was convicted and sentenced.

The dusters had claimed a victim.

However it didn't rest there. The Crown considered the six-month sentence to be inadequate for the crime and lodged an immediate appeal.

A bench of judges from the State's highest court heard the appeal. Reviewing the facts, they decided against increasing the sentence. Indeed, they found the appeal had taken so long, that the sentence was almost finished anyway.

The conviction was quashed, and Detective Bill was released from jail, thus ending one of the most bizarre molehill-to-mountain stories from Sydney's colourful inner-city police and criminal life.

PS It works out that Harold did not leave the knuckledusters in the van after all. Yes, it was all a mistake.

DEAR FATHER

Some unscrupulous operators will put money before anything else. In the case of this professional man even family was of secondary importance.

The lift doors opened and a grey-suited man walked out and straight to the secretary sitting at the small desk directly in front:

"Could you tell Mr Bagotti that John Smith from the Law Society is here for his appointment?"

The secretary asked John Smith to take a seat while she passed the message on.

In a few moments a short, rotund and balding man walked through a side door and strided across the floor with his left hand extended.

> *BAGOTTI:* Mr Smith! Good to put a face to the name. I've heard you've done some good work catching the naughty people in our profession. Just come through into the conference room.

John was led through what was little more than a passage which was lined on both sides with 1970s-style plywood-topped desks. There was not a word processor in sight. This was unusual for a solicitor's office. In fact the whole room seemed somewhat archaic.

There was only one person in the passage/room. A small man who looked remarkably like Mr Bagotti himself – although an aged version.

As John Smith walked past he saw the man was punching numbers into an adding machine which was obviously a relic of past days and methods. This man was working hard.

The conference room was much different. The centrepiece was beautiful wooden table. John Smith guessed it was oak – and not just Tasmanian oak. It was quite exotic.

Bagotti pressed a button on a panel on the table. The lavender vertical blinds separated, opening onto a view of the city, and the Brisbane River.

After messaging through an order for coffee, Bagotti sat down and invited his guest to sit opposite:

> *BAGOTTI:* So, Mr Smith. You told me on the phone that you needed help with an investigation. I'd be pleased to do what I can – barring any breaches of client confidentiality of course *(laughing)*. Who's in trouble?
>
> *SMITH: (Avoiding eye contact.)* Well, I don't know how to say this. It's *you* we have received a complaint against Mr Bagotti. One of your clients has alleged that your firm made a financial mess of her account.

John Smith quickly shuffled his papers, found the complaint, and read it out. At the end he looked up to see a very pale Spiros Bagotti.

The charming host suddenly turned into a cold and suspicious man on the defensive:

> *BAGOTTI:* And you believed this rubbish. . . ?
>
> *SMITH:* No. We're just investigating. . .
>
> *BAGOTTI:* Garbage. You Gestapo types don't investigate anything. You convict and try to roll heads. *(He stood.)* Go do your investigating. But just remember, if I find you or your henchmen have been slandering me, I'll sue. And I'll win.

John Smith decided not to argue. In a case like this there was nothing to say. The department would have to subpoena Bagotti's records. It was a long process, but it had to be done.

A week later, John Smith was at his office desk in the investigations unit when a message came through that Spiros Bagotti was there to see him. John was surprised. He did not expect Bagotti to make any personal contact after the confrontation. In fact John had been waiting for a legal letter of some kind. But here was the little man himself. Some seconds later Bagotti walked into the office, loaded with files, and wearing that same smile that had greeted John at the beginning of their prior meeting.

SMITH: Mr Bagotti, I didn't expect to. . .

Bagotti continued his annoying habit of cutting off everything John tried to say:

BAGOTTI: No, No, I was angry that's all. I mean, the allegation was serious and placed a cloud over my practice – a practice I had built myself over twenty years. It was a blow, a shock. Pride is very important to me and my family. Ethics are the most important thing for a solicitor. I got defensive. I'm sorry.

SMITH: I see you've brought in your files.

BAGOTTI: Yes. Everything you want. But there's no need to bother. I've found the problem.

SMITH: (Treading carefully.) What problem are you talking about?

BAGOTTI: The one you brought up last time. You know – making a financial mess of that client's books. Yes, I must admit it happened. But it's okay.

SMITH: What do you mean?

BAGOTTI: I found out who made the mistake and I fired him.

SMITH: Mr Bagotti, we'll need to speak to this person. Who is he?

BAGOTTI: Oh, you don't need to speak to him. Besides he's likely to be furious with me for sacking him. He'd probably say anything to hurt me now. He was that old man sitting in the accounting room when you came to see me last week.

SMITH: (Persisting.) I will still need his name. . .

BAGOTTI: (After some more hesitation.) Roland. Roland Bagotti.

SMITH: (Smiling, making a joke.) Any relation?

BAGOTTI: Er, yes. He's my father.

SMITH: Your own father?

BAGOTTI: (Rushing through the papers.) Yes, stuffed up things good and proper. Here are the books. You wouldn't believe it would you. I brought him out of retirement so he wouldn't get bored and then he goes and does this to me. . .

It took John two weeks to track down Mr Bagotti senior. The books did not disclose who was in the wrong. The interview with Bagotti Senior, did.

The Solicitor's Tribunal was given all the evidence. Bagotti Junior, Bagotti Senior and John Smith all gave testimony. A handwriting expert was called in, as were witnesses from the client's firm. They all indicated that fault lay with the younger Bagotti.

At the end of a short deliberation, the panel found Bagotti Junior was the sole person responsible for the financial mess.

Father, they found, had carried out his work in a meticulous manner. In fact, they found that if it wasn't for Bagotti Senior, the firm would have been in trouble with its clients' accounts long ago.

Spiros Bagotti was struck off the legal roll.

John Smith sat in his office and looked at a piece of stationery – a letter sent to him by Bagotti Junior early in the investigation. The letterhead started:

ROLAND BAGOTTI (SOLICITOR) AND SON

So Bagotti Senior had started the firm, brought in his son and eventually transferred the whole practice to him. In return, he was slave-driven in his retirement and blamed for his son's own shortcomings.

Ain't parenthood grand. . .

THE GENEROUS MAN

People commit crimes for all sorts of reasons. The idea of the noble thief – one who steals to benefit others – goes back to the legend of Robin Hood. I was fortunate enough to cover a case of a latter-day Aussie Robin Hood.

Joan, an animated thirty-year-old, ran through the front door of her home and collided with her twin brother, who was about to exit through the same door. She forced him back, said she couldn't wait to tell him what had happened, and then said he'd never guess. The brother was used to his sibling's eccentric ways. She had worked in King's Cross far too long – the craziness of the local ways had become part of her character.

He patiently asked Joan to tell him what had happened. She ran into the kitchen, repeating that he'd never guess, and that she was going to "put a cup of tea on".

He heard the water running and the crockery rattling. Joan then called out for him to look in the driveway. He obeyed.

There, just inside the gate, stood a shiny new sports car. Joan came to his side. Brother dear asked her if she had taken out the loan she was taking about.

No.

Well then, did the company give her a car. . .?

No.

She didn't steal it?

No.

Well whose was it?

Hers.

Over the cup of tea, Joan told her brother the unbelievable tale. . .

She was having lunch in the outdoor cafe just off Darlinghurst Road. This middle-aged respectable-looking man asked if he could eat at her table.

Over the next hour this man tells her all about himself. He says he is not trying to pick her up or anything. He shows her pictures of his wife and children.

Then he drops the bombshell. He has too much money.

He has inherited a fortune, and he's worried about how it's going to affect his children's lives. He then asks Joan if there is anything she wants – anything. No catches.

A car. A car would be nice.

No sooner said, than Joan and the man are headed for the car dealership around the corner. Joan points to the sports car, and this man goes with a saleswoman to handle the paperwork.

Everything goes like a dream. The sales staff say all the paperwork is in order. . . the man will make all the payments. In fact she could take the car right now. It's a demonstrator.

No demonstrator for this benefactor. He insists on a new car, but Joan says it's perfectly fine. . . she loves this car.

So the man shakes Joan's hand and wishes her well. He's glad to have been of help. His name is Alfred, by the way.

That same week, in a business office. . .

Alfred asked his secretary Bette if she would come into his office. Once inside he asked her to close the door and sit down.

Bette took this as a bad sign, and asked Alfred if she had done anything wrong.

Alfred smiled. Of course she hadn't done anything wrong. In fact she might be able to help him. He was in a bit of a bind.

He passed over a newspaper clipping showing a competition for a new car. He told her he had won the first prize – a sports car.

After the congratulations, Alfred explained he didn't need the car. He wanted to know if she would like it.

Bette replied she would have no way of paying him for a car like that. She was still paying off that used Commodore.

Alfred laughed, and told her he didn't want to *sell* her the car, he wanted to *give* it to her. A present for all the years of service she had given.

Bette said she couldn't accept such a large gift from the company. Alfred shook his head. No. It's not from the company – it's from him personally. . . a gift to Bette and her husband. Just one of life's little bonuses.

But there was one condition. . . don't go around telling everyone. Just enjoy it – it's like a symbol of how highly valued her work has been. Apart from that there are no catches.

Bette left the office in a daze. Alfred brought the car to work the next day. Bette drove it home.

Alfred called in at the company's regional headquarters and asked if he could see Greta, the young designer who had been with the firm for three years.

For years Greta had been promised high station and a good contract, but this hadn't eventuated. Alfred took an interest in Greta's development with the company, and thought it criminal that she had not been elevated to the status he believed she deserved.

A harried Greta came to the receptionist's desk and greeted Alfred. She was always glad to see him. He was like a caring uncle.

Alfred arranged for Greta to take an early lunch break. The pair drove to a nearby restaurant where, over oysters and Chardonnay, Alfred told her he had been promoted.

Greta was very happy for Alfred. She thought he deserved a better deal than he appeared to be getting with the company. But to her surprise, Alfred said he was now receiving *too much* money. He honestly didn't know what to do with it. That was why he called her to lunch. He wanted to share his good fortune with her.

He asked Greta if she liked the sports car they drove to the restaurant in. Greta said she sure did – and said one day she was going to have one just like it.

She dropped her spoon in the soup when Alfred told her that "one day" was today. It was hers, no catches.

Bette was sitting at her desk outside Alfred's office, reading the Car's Owner's Manual. She had had a lot of trouble setting the forty-five AM and FM stations on the car's multi-speaker 200-watt quadrophonic sound system. Three men appeared before her. They asked if Alfred was in. She said yes, and asked them their names and the nature of their visit.

The men told her they were from the Australian Securities Commission and had a warrant for Alfred's arrest on twenty counts of embezzlement.

Bette buzzed Alfred and pointed to his office door.

After the men closed the door, Bette threw the manual in the bin.

Alfred pleaded guilty to the twenty charges.

After further investigations, another 320 counts were laid.

All the cars were confiscated. They were the proceeds of crime, and were sold so the company could get back some of its embezzled money.

THE MORAL: Even when there's no catch, there's usually a catch. . .

SOMEONE UP THERE LIKES ME

This is a story of incredible luck. . . and the smallest of loopholes.

"All right Sergeant," the magistrate asked, "what wonderful tale do we have now?"

The sergeant stood up. He was wearing a double-breasted suit, and sported a Hollywood-style layered haircut. The magistrate grimaced each time he looked at him.

> *SERGEANT:* Charge case fifteen, Your Worship. Dennis Ring, Your Worship. Refusing to undergo a breathalyser test, Your Worship. The facts of the case, Your Worship are that on the evening. . .

The dapper young sergeant then told how Mr Ring had been booked for driving under the influence of alcohol after failing a roadside breath test.

The sergeant told the magistrate that Mr Ring had refused to undergo the computerised breathalyser test at the police station. . . well sort of.

The magistrate raised his eyebrows.

> *MAGISTRATE:* Sergeant, how does one "sort of" refuse a breathalyser test? Did he take the test?
>
> *SERGEANT:* Yes, Your Worship.
>
> *MAGISTRATE:* Well, there's your answer. He did not refuse.
>
> *SERGEANT:* He *did* refuse.

The magistrate took off his glasses. He was annoyed.

MAGISTRATE: What the hell are you talking about, Sergeant?

Dennis remembered the night very clearly as the sergeant told the story. The fright of being arrested had sobered Dennis up. When he arrived at the station, he was taken into a small room, where he was told he was being charged for mid-range PCA (prescribed concentration of alcohol) after failing the roadside breath test.

Dennis was asked to sit down. The sergeant explained about the huge computerised breathalyser machine. Dennis was then asked if he understood the instructions.

"Okay. Now blow through the tube."

Dennis' mind raced at a hundred miles an hour. Blimey. Maybe he was way over the limit. What could he do? What to do? What to do?

Looking at the tube, the obvious dawned upon him. He blew, but not very hard. He puffed out his cheeks feigning great effort.

"Okay Sir. That's enough."

Dennis put the tube down and awaited verdict. The sergeant seemed puzzled. Then he slowly looked at his charge.

"You didn't blow very hard, did you?"

Dennis was indignant. "What me? It must be your machine."

The sergeant drew a slow, deep breath. He fitted a new tube and handed it to Dennis with an order to re-breathe.

Dennis was well prepared to repeat the deep-breath facade, when the sergeant added that failure to follow orders brought automatic disqualification.

Fear was replaced by resignation. Dennis' only wish now was to get it over with. Que sera. For what it was worth Dennis asked his Maker for a little assistance. He then gave a full breath, and slumped back into his seat.

After a minute he looked up, expecting to see the sergeant grinning knowingly and taking down vindictive statistics from the machine. Instead, the sergeant had the same puzzled expression.

"The bloody thing's not working."

Dennis almost didn't hear the words. The magic words.

"Not a bloody thing."

Dennis sent thanks to Those Above.

"What will I bloody do now?"

Dennis sent more thanks to Those Above, and gave a PS: please let me be released from custody.

"You'll have to do it again, sport."

Righteousness and indignation combined.

"No bloody way, mate. You've had your chance. You screwed up. I did my bit. I blew. Twice. I'm not going to sit here until bloody Christmas, blowing away until you get it right."

The sergeant looked down at the machine, and gave it a hit on the side, hoping for a miracle – something like Dennis' miracle. It didn't happen.

The sergeant asked Dennis again. Dennis refused again.

The sergeant rested his chin on his palm. He couldn't charge Dennis with drink-driving. He didn't have the conclusive proof. The roadside "blow in the bag" test wouldn't stand up in court.

A constable walked in the room. "How's it going sarge? Taking a bit of a while?"

"Yeah. The bloody machine's on the blink."

"Try it again."

"Yeah, but he won't do it a-bloody-gen."

"Did you try hitting it on the side?"

"Yeah, tried that."

A short conference followed. It was then decided to charge Dennis with refusing to take the breath test.

Dennis had been confident of the outcome. They would decide he was a bloody nuisance, and order him off the premises with the customary warnings. Instead Dennis left with a piece of paper with something about bail conditions on it.

The magistrate had listened closely as the events were told to the court.

After a pause, Dennis was asked if he had representation. Before he could answer, his solicitor jumped from a seat on the side of the court and strode to a vacant chair near the suited sergeant.

SOLICITOR: Yes, Your Worship. Howe. Your Worship. From the firm of Steele Moore Munney and Howe.

MAGISTRATE: Well what do you have to say about the charge?

Mr Howe slapped his designer briefcase on the table, took out two documents, and looked at them. He looked up to see the magistrate staring at him.

HOWE: Excuse me just a moment, Your Worship.

The dapper solicitor turned and motioned to Dennis, who, ever eager to help with the detail in the case, dashed over to his spokesperson's side:

DENNIS: (Whispering.) What do you need, Mr Howe?

HOWE: You should've blown in the machine. You drink drivers make it very difficult, you know.

DENNIS: But I. . .

HOWE: Never mind. I'll do my best. You can sit here. If I say anything wrong, let me know.

The young solicitor slammed his hands on the briefcase, shut it, and moved it to the floor, every movement of significance.

HOWE: Your Worship. You've heard the evidence. I submit that this man... *(His arm made a wide sweep across to Dennis.)* That this man did all that was legally required of him. He did not refuse to give a breath at the roadside. He submitted to arrest. He blew into the computer breathalyser at the station. He was happy to do these things. He wanted to do them. His name was at stake. He is a reputable professional person in this area. He wanted to ensure that the police would realise their error quickly, and then release him to go on his way. Your Worship, I ask you honestly, how could this man *(sweep re-enacted)* be charged with refusing to undergo a test. He had agreed twice. Twice, Your Worship. Twice. I ask that the charge not only be dismissed, but exiled from this court with the scorn and derision it deserves.

Exhausted, Mr Howe resumed his seat. The magistrate had been pleasantly surprised. Drama was so rare in this court. He liked the odd bit of flair in advocacy.

He tapped his fingers on the desk, not to help decide the issue, but to phrase his finding in a way which would not be upstaged by Howe's speech. He tapped for a while.

MAGISTRATE: As I see this case, this fellow agreed to undergo the test. If I convict Mr... Mr... Mr... *(he scrambled for the charge sheets)* Ring... for refusing to undergo a test, there's no telling where the case could end. If he refused the forty-seventh time, should he then be charged? No. That's not fair.

The magistrate then threw the case out.

As Dennis left the court, the sergeant walked up to him and said, "We're going to appeal, sport".

Dennis smiled and walked out into the sunshine. He was free again. No charges. Let 'em appeal. I'll be right. Someone up there likes me.

The sergeant watched Dennis walk down the street. A little man who had beaten the system. The officer shook his head.

Someone up there must really like him.